The Complete

Anti-Inflammatory
Cookbook for Beginners

1200 Days of Affordable & Easy Recipes to Reduce your
Body Inflammation | 30 Days Meal Plan Included!

Marie S Rodriguez

CONTENTS

Introduction   4

What is and Anti-Inflammatory Diet and How Does It Work   4

How to Relieve Inflammation with Your Diet   4

Vegetables Mains   6

Fish and Seafood   25

Poultry   42

Sides, Salads and Soups   58

Breakfast   75

Fruits and Desserts   95

Sauces, Dips and Dressings   108

5-Weeks Meal Plan   116

Alphabetic Index   121

Introduction

WHAT IS AN ANTI-INFLAMMATORY DIET AND HOW DOES IT WORK

The anti-inflammatory diet is a diet aimed at counteracting the inflammatory processes and oxidative stress characteristic of many lifestyle-related chronic degenerative diseases such as type 2 diabetes mellitus, cardio-vascular disease, certain cancers, joint wear and tear, etc.

Oxidative stress can be defined as a disturbance in the ratio of antioxidant molecules to pro-oxidant molecules in favour of the latter, potentially causing cellular damage.
Excessive oxidative stress can exceed the body's capacity for antioxidation, thus promoting inflammatory mechanisms.

Inflammation - acute and chronic - is a process mediated by different tissues and immune factors, and may have different "dimensions" and "characteristics" depending on the case. Severe inflammations trigger definite reactions and often have obvious causes.
Then there is a mild or partial form of inflammation, which sometimes goes unnoticed until its consequences appear, but which should not be under-estimated, and which underlies problems such as atherosclerosis, certain joint degenerations, and so on.

Several theories establish a close link between autoimmune complications and chronic systemic inflammation. To date, the link is recognized but not fully understood, i.e., it is not clear what is the cause and what is the effect - probably the relationship runs both ways.

The essential principle of anti-inflammatory nutrition is to increase the molecules that can protect us from oxidative stress and positively influence systemic inflammation

HOW TO RELIEVE INFLAMMATION WITH YOUR DIET

The change in inflammatory parameters described above can be prevented or offset by the following dietary measures:
If overweight, achieving normal weight: after calorie reduction (low-calorie diet) and motor training (motor protocol for the treatment of obesity); If necessary, restoring the balance of the lipid fraction: reducing saturated fats in favour of unsaturated fats, limiting the intake of arachidonic acid and increasing the intake of omega-3 polyunsaturated fatty acids, especially eicosapentaenoic acid (EPA) and docosahexaenoic acid (DHA); If deficient, increase intake of essential antioxidant nutrients: Vitamin E or alpha-tocopherol, Vitamin C, carotenoids, zinc and selenium; Increase the intake of foods with antioxidant activity: these are all foods whose composition ensures antioxidant activity independent of essential nutrients.

These are mainly polyphenols, which are abundant in vegetables, etc. Attention. This does not mean that foods of animal origin do not contain non-vitamin or mineral antioxidants. Meat and fish, for example, contain abundant lipoic acid and coenzyme Q10. However, due to their general nutrient composition, they are not suitable for the anti-inflammatory diet.

PREPARATION FOR THE ANTI-INFLAMMATORY DIET: WHAT TO AVOID

The theory of the anti-inflammatory diet is that certain foods may increase systemic inflammation. However, important academic studies refute this hypothesis. It is undeniable, however, that:
A deficiency of vitamins and minerals that play a role in combating oxidative stress, and an insufficient intake of other natural antioxidants (such as many polyphenols). contribute massively to increased oxidative stress.

Excess arachidonic acid, if not balanced by proper levels of omega-3 fatty acids, increases inflammation and cardiovascular risk

Obesity contributes to increased parameters of chronic inflammation, but the link with junk food is indirect; Anyway, let us make a short list of foods that can increase oxidative stress and inflammation according to the anti-inflammatory diet:

- Refined carbohydrates, such as white bread and sweets;
- French fries and other fried foods;
- Lemonade and other sugary drinks;
- Red (hamburgers, steaks) and processed meats (hot dogs, sausages);
- Margarine, lard, and lard.

On the other hand, what foods reduce inflammation?

Even for foods that reduce oxidative stress and inflammation, the scientific evidence offers only incomplete or interpretable results. For example:

Phytocomplexes objectively have an antioxidant effect;
However, in healthy people, increasing their proportion in the diet does not lead to a change in parameters related to inflammation. Therefore, the anti-inflammatory diet could be a useful measure only for people who do not eat fruits and vegetables. A person who already consumes the portions recommended for a healthy, balanced diet would not benefit. Let us go back to a short list of foods that the anti-inflammatory diet says could reduce oxidative stress and inflammation:
Tomatoes;
Olive oil;

Green leafy vegetables, such as spinach, and kale of different varieties (daughter and flower);
Walnuts, hazelnuts and almonds;
Oily fish, salmon and other cold-water fish.

Some fruits, such as strawberries, blueberries, cherries and oranges; an Examples of anti-inflammatory food correction. The following is an example of an anti-inflammatory food correction:
- 5 servings of vegetables and fruits with high antioxidant activity (e.g. berries, red plums, spinach, broccoli, etc.);
- 2 servings of hot drinks such as coffee, tea and chocolate;
- 1 serving of 200 ml of a beverage such as orange juice, juice mix (orange, carrot, lemon), etc.; and 1-2 glasses of red wine;
- Extra virgin olive oil.

In a person who has high levels of C-reactive protein, such a diet can help lower the levels.

6 RULES FOR ALWAYS PICKING HEALTHY FOOD

1. Do not eat anything that your great-grandmother would not recognize as food
Always read the ingredients composing what you are going to eat. Prefer food with fewer ingredients.

2. Avoid foods that list any form of sugar or sweetener among the first three ingredients
Sugar causes severe inflammation.

3. Don't buy food where you buy your gasoline.
20% of meals are eaten in the car. You should only eat at your table not at a desk while working, watching television or driving.

4. Eat food that is cooked by people, not corporations
Prefer wholesome food and meals you know where they come from

5. Eat animals that have fed themselves well
Carefully chose your meat. Reduce consumption and increase quality control.

6. Buy fresh food from the farmer's market whenever possible

Vegetables Mains

Fennel and Pumpkin Riso...

Cooking Time | Serving

1 hour   4

- 360 g risotto rice
- 450 g pumpkin
- 350 g fennel
- 4 tablespoons extra virgin olive oil
- 40g leek
- vegetable stock to taste
- salt to taste
- Pepper to taste
- Parsley to taste

First, cut the pumpkin into small cubes, c the fennel and slice the leek;

In the meantime, prepare a vegetable broth

Put the oil in a pan, add the leek and fry it lig before adding the vegetables;

Then add the diced vegetables and cook o medium heat, adding broth as needed, u the vegetables are well cooked and tender will take about20 minutes);

Season with salt and pepper;

Add the riwce to the vegetables, then gradu add the broth and stir everything toget Pour in the boiling broth slowly as the cooks, adding the next ladleful when the has well absorbed the previous broth;

After about 20 minutes, the vegetables sh have melted and formed a fragrant cream, the rice should be cooked just right;

Transfer to a plate and serve with fre chopped parsley.

Cabbage, Quinoa and Avocado Salad

Cooking Time | Serving

40 min   3

- 1 sweet potato, peeled and cut into pieces
- 2 teaspoons of olive oil
- 1 avocado
- 1 tablespoon lime juice
- 1 clove of garlic
- 1/8 teaspoon salt
- 1-2 tablespoons of water
- 1 cup of cooked quinoa
- 1 cup canned black beans
- 1 cup shredded cabbage
- 1 shallot, chopped

We start by preheating the oven to 400 degrees F°.

Next, we arranged the sweet potatoes and 1 tablespoon of oil on a large rimmed baking sheet. We place them in the oven and let them roast, stirring once halfway through cooking, until tender. We keep it in the oven for about 30 minutes.

Meanwhile, combine the remaining oil, avocado, lime juice, garlic, salt, pepper, and 1 tablespoon of water in a blender or food processor; process until smooth. Add 1 tablespoon of water, if necessary, to achieve the desired consistency.

At this point, to finish the recipe, combine the sweet potato, quinoa, black beans, and kale in a medium bowl. Add the previously created dressing to the dish and gently stir to coat everything.

Calories | Protein | Fat | Carbs |

Calories	Protein	Fat	Carbs
450	15.5g	19g	62.4g

Vegetarian Carbonara

Cooking Time | Serving

25 min

4

300 gr. whole grain fusilli or gluten-free fusilli,
4 carrots,
2 fennel (the most tender part),
2 celery stalks,
1 shallot,
6 cabbage leaves,
3 tablespoons of extra virgin olive oil,
3 eggs,
a small pinch of nutmeg,
salt and pepper to taste

Wash the carrots and fennel and cut them into julienne strips. Wash the celery and cabbage leaves and cut them into thin strips and the shallot, after peeling, into small pieces.

Fry all the vegetables in a large pan with hot oil for two minutes, then add a pinch of salt and cover with a lid.

Cook for another 15 minutes over low heat. Meanwhile, cook the pasta in a pot with plenty of lightly salted boiling water.

Whisk the eggs in a bowl with grated nutmeg, salt, and pepper. Pour the pasta al dente and save a few ladles of the cooking water.

Add the pasta to the pot, the vegetables, 2 tablespoons of the cooking water, and the beaten eggs, and stir everything for a few seconds over low heat.

Serve immediately at the table.

Celery Turnip and Artichoke Soup Creme

Cooking Time | Serving

45 min

2

- 1 celery Rapa
- 4 carrots
- 1/2 leek
- 1 bay leaf
- 2 sage leaves
- grated goat cheese
- pink salt
- extra virgin coconut oil

Wash and peel the celeriac, then cut it into small pieces.

Clean the artichokes, remove the inner stubble and the harder outer leaves except for the most yellow and tender ones, and cut them into thin slices.

In a saucepan, sauté the chopped vegetables and the thinly sliced leeks with two tablespoons of coconut oil, the bay leaf, and the sage.

When they're golden brown, continue cooking them, adding half a cup of water for about 30 minutes (the vegetables should be well cooked, check by poking the celeriac with the tip of a fork).

When the vegetables are cooked, puree them until they're creamy.

Serve the soup in a dish with some grated cheese.

Savoy Cabbage Lasagna with Porcini Mushroom

Cooking Time | Serving

25-90 min

- **12 outer leaves of savoy cabbage**
- **600 gr celeriac**
- **100 gr grated goat's cheese.**
- **50 gr dried porcini mushrooms**
- **2 shrimp**
- **1 leek**
- **1 clove of garlic**
- **pepper**
- **almond butter**
- **rose salt**
- **extra virgin coconut oil**

Soak the dried mushrooms in a cup of hot water for at least 10 minutes.
Lasagna:
Fill a large pot with water and put it on the stove.
When the water boils, immerse the cabbage leaves and let them cook fe minutes.
Take the leaves out of the water, be careful not to burn them, and place them cotton towel to dry.
Save the cooking water from the cabbage.
The ragout - 1st step:
In a non-stick frying pan with 2 tablespoons of coconut oil, fry the light part thinly sliced leek, and then add the peeled celery turnip cut into small pieces.
Fry the stir fry, and then add the saved cabbage cooking water until the leek celery are generously covered and cook for about 15 minutes. Turn off the hea Put the leeks in a bowl.
Take the celeriac out of the pan, whisk it into a cream, and set aside. Sav cooking water from the leeks and celeriac.
The ragout - 1st step:
In a non-stick frying pan with 2 tablespoons of coconut oil, fry the light part leek, cut into thin slices and then add the celeriac peeled and cut into small pi Fry the stir fry and then add the cabbage cooking water that you've saved ur leeks and celery are generously covered and cook for about 15 minutes.
Turn off the heat.
Put the leeks in a bowl.
Take the celeriac out of the pan, whisk it into a cream, and set aside.
Save the cooking water from the leeks and celeriac.
Step 2:
In another pan with 2 tablespoons of coconut oil, fry the sliced shallot, the p and chopped mushrooms, the garlic clove, and the diced cabbage.
Once they're golden brown, add the cooking water of the leek and celery ane for about 15 minutes.
When the latter vegetables are cooked, add them to the bowl with the leeks.
In an oiled baking dish (or with baking paper on the bottom), arrange a la cabbage leaves, celeriac, ragout, goat cheese, butter flakes, and pepper.
Alternate the layers as described above until you run out of ingredients.

Pasta with Savoy Cabbage and Cheese

Cooking Time | Serving

90 min   5

- **For The Dough:**
- **350 Gr Saracen Wheat Flour.**
- **150 Gr Quinoa Flour.**
- **250 Ml Water**
- **2 Pinches Of Pink Salt**
- **For The Dressing:**
- **1 Small Sauce (About 250-300 Gr)**
- **1 Clove Of Garlic**
- **2 Sage Leaves**
- **100 Gr Malga Butter.**
- **Grated Goat Cheese**
- **Uncooked Goat Cheese**

Prepare the dough:
Mix the flours in a big bowl.
Add the water and knead it until you have a firm ball.
When the dough is ready, wrap it in plastic and leave it to rest for 30 minutes.
Roll out the dough on a board with a rolling pin until you get a sheet about 2 to 3 mm thick, and cut the fresh dough into about 5-6 cm wide strips.
Dust the resulting strips with flour and cut them overlapping into 1 cm wide noodles.
For the topping:
Wash the savoy cabbage well and cut it into thin slices.
Cook the savoy cabbage in boiling water with 1 tablespoon salt for about 10 minutes.
Then add the pasta and cook for 10 more minutes.
At the end of the cooking time, arrange a layer of noodles and savoy cabbage
In a hot casserole dish with a skimmer, sprinkle the goat cheese in flakes.
Then make another layer of pasta, savoy cabbage, and more goat cheese until you run out of them.
Melt the butter in a small pan with the garlic clove and sage and pour it over the hot pasta.
Serve at the table.

dian Spinach Soup with Crunchy Bread

Cooking Time | Serving

25 min   1 cup

4 ounces paneer cheese, cut into 1/2-inch cubes.
¼ teaspoon ground turmeric
1 tablespoon extra virgin olive oil, divided.
half small onion, finely diced
1 jalapeño pepper, finely chopped (optional)
1 clove of garlic, chopped
1 tablespoon chopped fresh ginger
1 teaspoon garam masala
1/2 teaspoon ground cumin
10 ounces frozen spinach, thawed and finely chopped
1/4 teaspoon salt
1 cup low-fat plain yogurt

Mix the paneer with turmeric in a medium bowl until coated—heat 1 tablespoon of oil in a large skillet over medium heat.

Add the paneer to the pan and flip it once until brown cooked on both sides. Transfer to a plate. Add the remaining 1 tablespoon of oil to the skillet. Add onion and jalapeño and frequently stir until golden brown, 7 to 8 minutes. (If the pan seems dry, add water (2 tablespoons at a time). Add garlic, ginger, garam masala, and cumin.

Stir for 30 seconds. Add spinach and salt. After 3 minutes, remove from heat and stir in yogurt and paneer.

lories	Protein	Fat	Carbs	Fiber	Sodium	Cholesterol
384	22.5 g	22.3 g	20.9 g	4.3 g	640 mg	62.1 g

Chickpeas and Cauliflower Casserole

Cooking Time | Serving

40 min   2-4

- 10 oz canned chickpeas, drained (see notes for substitutes).
- 1/2 lb cauliflower florets (about 2-3 cups).
- 1+ teaspoon curry seasoning or 1 tablespoon curry sauce of your choice
- 1/4 teaspoon garlic powder or 1 teaspoon minced garlic
- 1 tablespoon olive oil
- kosher salt and pepper to taste
- 2 cups cooked rice or cauliflower rice (you can combine to taste)
- An optional handful of spinach or other leafy greens

Prepare the oven to 175 degrees and grease a casserole dish (12x8 is preferred) or glass container.

Sauté chickpeas and cauliflower in curry powder and 1 tablespoon of oil. Add kosher salt and pepper.

Layer the cooked rice or cauliflower rice (or a mixture of both) on the bottom of your casserole dish, then layer the chickpeas and cauliflower on top of it.

Add spinach or herbs to the rice/cauliflower and sprinkle it with parmesan cheese.

Bake it for 25-30 minutes. (After baking, you can freeze it for up to 3 months). Sprinkle the casserole with additional curry, garlic, pepper, lemon slices, etc., before serving.

Calories	Protein	Fat	Carbs	Fiber	Sodium	Sugar
282	9.6g	3.9g	53g	6.8	462	1.4g

Casserole with Green Bea

Cooking Time | Serving

55 min

- 1 bag of frozen whole green beans
- cooking spray oil
- 2 bowls of mushrooms (chopped)
- 60 g onion (diced)
- 1 clove of garlic (chopped)
- 180 g Greek yogurt (low fat)
- 60 g sour cream (low fat)
- 1 teaspoon cornstarch
- 1/2 sachet stevia
- 1/2 teaspoon salt
- 1/2 teaspoon black pepper
- 1/2 bowl grated cheddar cheese (low fat)
- 2 tablespoons grated Parmesan cheese

Preheat the oven to 180°C.
Prepare the green beans in the microw
according to the instructions on the packag
Lightly grease a frying pan and heat o
medium heat. Cook mushrooms, onions,
garlic until tender (about 5-7 minutes). Mix
mushroom mixture with the green beans
bowl and let cool.
Whisk together Greek yogurt, sour cre
cornstarch, stevia, salt, and black pepper
bowl. Stir the vegetables into the sauce mix
until smooth. Add the cheddar cheese and
in until everything is well blended.
Spread in a lightly greased baking dish, spri
with parmesan and bake until golden bro
(about 30-35 minutes).

Tomato Basil Soup

Cooking Time | Serving

25 min   2

- 240 g tomatoes, diced
- 1/2 bowl with water
- 240 g basil leaves
- 1 tablespoon low-sodium, low-fat cheese, grated

Put the tomatoes in a pot and pour the water. Close the lid.
Turn the heat to medium and let the tomatoes simmer.
Puree the tomatoes with a hand blender while still in the pot.
Add the basil leaves and cook for another 2 minutes.
Arrange in bowls and serve with 1/2 tablespoon grated cheese.

Calories | Protein | Fat | Carbs | Sugar |

Calories	Protein	Fat	Carbs	Sugar
137	1.7g	0.9g	3g	0.9g

auliflower Salad

Cooking Time | Serving

18 min   2

240 g cauliflower florets
60 g apple cider vinegar
1 tablespoon Tuscan dressing

Put all the ingredients in a bowl and mix.
Leave in the refrigerator for at least 30 minutes
before serving.

lories | Protein | Fat | Carbs | Sugar |

41   1.3g   0.1g   8.7g   2g

Lean Green Broccoli Tacos

Cooking Time | Serving

30 min   4

- 120 g 95-97% lean ground beef
- 60 Roma tomatoes, diced
- 1/4 teaspoon garlic powder
- 1/4 teaspoon onion powder
- 300 g broccoli, chopped
- A pinch of red bell pepper flakes
- 30 g low-sodium cheddar cheese, grated

Put 3 tablespoons of water in a pan and heat it over medium heat. Sauté the beef and tomatoes for 5 minutes until the tomatoes wilted.
Add the garlic and onion powder and sauté for another 3 minutes.
Add the broccoli and close the lid. Cook for another 5 minutes.
Garnish with red bell pepper flakes and cheddar cheese.

Calories | Protein | Fat | Carbs | Sugar

97   9.9g   1.7g   2.6g   0.9g

Vegetables and Mushrooms Wr

Cooking Time | Serving

40 min   3

- Piquant glazed mushrooms:
- 1/2 teaspoon olive oil
- 1/2 (10- to 12-ounce / 284- to 340-g) package Cremini mushrooms, rinsed and drained, thinly sliced
- ½ teaspoon chili powder
- Sea salt and freshly ground black pepper to taste
- 1/2 teaspoon maple syrup
- Fajitas:
- 1 teaspoon olive oil
- 1/2 onion, diced
- Sea salt, to taste
- 1/2 pepper, any color, seeded and cut into julienne
- 1/2 zucchini, cut into large sticks
- 3 whole wheat tortillas
- 1 carrot, grated
- 2 spring onions, sliced
- 1/4 cup fresh coriander, finely chopped

Prepare spicy glazed mushrooms

Heat the olive oil in a non-stick frying pan medium heat

Add the mushrooms and sauté for 10 minutes.

Sprinkle the mushrooms with chili powder, salt, ground black pepper.

Drizzle with maple syrup. Stir well and cook for 5 minutes. Set aside.

Make the tortilla

Put the olive oil in a pan over medium heat.

Add the onion and heat until translucent, sprinkle with salt.

Add the pepper and zucchini and fry them minutes until they're soft.

Meanwhile, toast the tortilla in the oven fe minutes.

Let the tortilla cool for a few minutes, then fil tortilla with the glazed mushrooms and vegeta

Serve immediately.

Calories	Protein	Fat	Carbs	Fiber	Sodiu
43	11.2g	14.8g	7.9g	7.0g	230m

Vegetable Pita

Cooking Time | Serving

10 min   8

- 1 cup baby spinach leaves
- 1 small red onion, thinly sliced
- 1 small cucumber, seeded and cut into pieces
- 2 tomatoes, diced
- 2 cups chopped romaine lettuce
- 2 tablespoons extra virgin olive oil
- 1 tablespoon red wine vinegar
- 2 teaspoon Dijon mustard
- 2 tablespoon crumbled feta cheese
- Sea salt and freshly ground pepper, to taste
- 2 whole wheat pita

Mix all the ingredients, except the pita, in a large bowl.

Fill the pita with the salad and serve immediately.

Calories	Protein	Fat	Carbs	Fiber	Sodium
137	3.1g	8.1g	14.3g	2.4g	166mg

Vegetarian Burgers

Cooking Time | Serving

2 hours   3

1/2 tablespoon avocado oil
1/2 yellow onion, diced
1/4 cup grated carrots
2 garlic cloves, halved
1/2 can (215 g) of black beans, rinsed and drained
1/2 cup gluten-free rolled oats
1/8 cup oil-packed sun-dried tomatoes, drained and diced
1/4 cup sunflower seeds, toasted
1/2 teaspoon paprika powder
1/2 teaspoon ground cumin seeds
1/4 cup fresh parsley, stems removed
1/8 teaspoon ground red pepper flakes
3/8 teaspoon sea salt
1/8 teaspoon ground black pepper
1/8 cup olive oil
To serve
3 wholemeal rolls, halved and toasted
1 ripe avocado, cut into slices
1/2 cup of kaiser sprouts or mung bean sprouts
1/2 ripe tomato, sliced

Heat avocado oil in a non-stick pan over medium heat.
Add the onion and carrots and cook for 10 minutes.
Add the garlic.
After 30 seconds, please put it in a food processor and add the remaining ingredients, except the olive oil. Blend until everything is chopped and the mixture holds together. Be careful not to over-blend the mixture.
Divide the mixture and form into six burgers, 5 cm in diameter and 0.5 cm thick.
Place the burgers on a baking sheet and wrap them in plastic wrap. Place the baking sheet in the refrigerator and freeze for at least an hour. Then take the baking sheet out of the fridge and let them rest at room temperature for 10 minutes.
Heat the olive oil in a non-stick skillet over medium-high heat until shimmering.
Cook the patties in the pan until lightly browned and crispy. Turn the burgers halfway through the cooking time. You may need to work in multiple layers to avoid overcrowding.
Top the buns with patties, avocados, sprouts, and tomato slices.

Calories | Protein | Fat | Carbs | Fiber | Sodium |

Calories	Protein	Fat	Carbs	Fiber	Sodium
613	26.2g	23.1g	88.3g	22.9g	456mg

Vegetarian Pita

Cooking Time | Serving

15 min   8

- 3 cup seedless cucumbers, peeled and diced
- 2 cups chopped tomato
- 1 cup finely chopped fresh mint
- 1/2 cup diced red onion
- 2 can (2.25 oz / 64 g) sliced black olives, drained
- 4 tablespoons extra virgin olive oil
- 2 tablespoon red wine vinegar
- 1/2 teaspoon kosher salt
- 1/2 teaspoon freshly ground black pepper
- 1 cup crumbled goat cheese
- 8 whole wheat flatbread wraps or soft whole wheat tortillas

Combine the cucumber, tomato, mint, onion, and olives in a bowl.
Beat together the oil, vinegar, salt, and pepper.
Spread the dressing over the salad. Toss gently to mix everything together.
Place the wraps on a clean work surface. Spread the goat cheese evenly over the wraps.
Scoop a quarter of the salad into the center of each pita.
Fold up each wrap as a cylinder.
Enjoy

Calories | Protein | Fat | Carbs | Fiber | Sodium |

Calories	Protein	Fat	Carbs	Fiber	Sodium
225	12g	12g	18g	4g	349mg

Stuffed potato

Cooking Time | Serving

50 min   4

- 2 small potatoes
- 1/2 teaspoon coconut oil
- 1/2 small onion, finely chopped
- 1/2 small piece ginger, minced
- 1 garlic clove, minced
- 1 to 2 teaspoons curry powder
- Sea salt and freshly ground black pepper to taste
- ¼ cup frozen peas, thawed
- 1 carrot, grated
- ¼ cup chopped fresh cilantro

Prepare the oven to 350ºF (180ºC).
Poke potatoes with a fork making small h
then wrap them in aluminum foil.
Bake for 30 minutes.
Meanwhile, melt the coconut oil into a nons
skillet.
Add the onion and cook until translucent.
Add the ginger and garlic and sauté
fragrant.
Add the curry powder, salt, and black pep
then stir.
When 30 minutes have passed, remove
potatoes from the foil and slice them in hal
Hollow potato halves with a spoon, then mi
potato with onion, peas, carrots, and cilant
a large bowl. Stir to combine well.
Spoon the mixture back to the potato skins
serve immediately

Calories | Protein | Fat | Carbs | Fiber | Sodiu

Calories	Protein	Fat	Carbs	Fiber	Sodium
131	3.2g	13.9g	8.8g	3.0g	111m

Vegetarian Sandwich

Cooking Time | Serving

18 min   4

- 2 medium eggplant, sliced into ½- inch-thick slices
- 4 tablespoons olive oil
- Sea salt and freshly ground pepper, to taste
- 10 tablespoons hummus
- 8 slices of whole-wheat bread, toasted
- 2 cups baby spinach leaves
- 4 ounces (114 g) feta cheese, softened

Salt both sides of the sliced eggplant and let sit for 30 minutes, then pat them to dry.
Brush the slices with olive oil and add more sea salt and freshly ground pepper.
Grill the eggplant for 3 minutes on each side
Spread the hummus on the bread slices and top with the spinach leaves, feta, and eggplant slices.
Top the sandwich and enjoy!

Calories | Protein | Fat | Carbs | Fiber | Sodium |

Calories	Protein	Fat	Carbs	Fiber	Sodium
490	19.1g	24.3g	48.9g	16.7g	739mg

Mexican Sandwiches

Cooking Time | Serving

10 min   4

3/2 cup olive oil, divided
4 romaine lettuce hearts, left intact
6 to 8 anchovy fillets
Juice of 1 big lemon
4 to 6 cloves garlic, peeled
2 teaspoon Dijon mustard
1/2 teaspoon Worcestershire sauce
Sea salt and freshly ground pepper, to taste
4 slices of whole-wheat bread, toasted
Freshly grated Parmesan cheese for serving

Set medium heat and preheat the grill, and oil the grates.
Finely cut the lettuce and season with 4 tablespoons of olive oil
Mix the remaining olive oil with anchovies, lemon juice, garlic, mustard, and Worcestershire in a food processor.
Mix the ingredients until you have a smooth emulsion. Season with sea salt and pepper.
Place the lettuce, and the dressing on the bread, then sprinkle with parmesan cheese
Serve your dinner, and enjoy!

Calories	Protein	Fat	Carbs	Fiber	Sodium
939	14.9g	83.6g	32.1g	19.9g	721mg

Vegan Sandwiches

Cooking Time | Serving

20 min   4

- Dressing:
- 2 (30-ounce / 850-g) can cannellini beans, drained and rinsed
- 2/3 cup packed fresh basil leaves
- 2/3 cup packed fresh parsley
- 2/3 cup chopped fresh chives
- 4 garlic cloves, chopped
- Zest and juice of ½ lemon
- 2 tablespoons apple cider vinegar
- Sandwiches:
- 8 whole-grain bread slices, toasted
- 16 English cucumber slices
- 2 large beefsteak tomatoes, cut into slices
- 2 large avocados, halved, pitted, and cut into slices
- 2 small yellow bell pepper, cut into slices
- 4 handfuls of broccoli sprouts
- 4 handfuls of fresh spinach

In a food processor, combine the cannellini beans, basil, parsley, chives, garlic, lemon zest and juice, and vinegar. Purée until smooth.
Refrigerate for at least 1 hour to allow the flavors to blend.
Build sandwiches by layering two slices of bread with the cucumber, tomato, avocado, bell pepper, broccoli sprouts, and spinach.
Enjoy!

Calories	Protein	Fat	Carbs	Fiber	Sodium
617	30.1g	28.1g	99.1g	25.6g	580mg

Vegan Chickpea Wra

Cooking Time | Serving
15 min   4

- 2 (30 oz / 850g) can chickpeas, drained and rinsed well
- 2 celery stalk, diced
- 1 shallot, minced
- 2 green apple, cored and diced
- 6 tablespoons tahini (sesame paste)
- 4 teaspoons freshly squeezed lemon juice
- 2 teaspoon raw honey
- 2 teaspoon Dijon mustard
  Dash salt
- Filtered water, to thin
- 8 romaine lettuce leaves

Mix all the ingredients with a cup of water place the romaine lettuce leaves on a plate. Fill each with the chickpea filling, using it a Wrap the leaves around the filling. Se immediately.

Calories | Protein | Fat | Carbs | Fiber | Sodiu
Calories	Protein	Fat	Carbs	Fiber	Sodium
394	15.4g	15.4g	54.4g	14.4g	413mg

Vegan Burritos

Cooking Time | Serving
55 min   3

- 1/2 teaspoon olive oil
- 1/2 red onion, diced
- 1 garlic cloves, minced
- 1/2 zucchini, chopped
- 1/2 tomato, diced
- 1/2 bell pepper, any color, deseeded and diced
- 1/2 (7-ounce / 148-g) can black-eyed peas
- 1 teaspoons chili powder
- Sea salt, to taste
- 3 whole-grain tortillas

Prepare your oven to 325ºF
Put the olive oil in a pan over medium heat.
Add the onion and fry until traslucent (2 minutes).
Add the garlic for 30 seconds. Then sauté the zucchini for 5 minutes.
Add the tomato and bell pepper and sauté for 2 minutes.
Add the peas and mix well with chili powder and salt.
Place the tortillas on a surface, and fill them with the vegetables. Fold one ends of tortillas then tuck and roll them into burritos.
Put the burritos in a baking dish, then pour the remaining vegetables juice over the burritos.
Bake for 25 minutes.
Serve immediately.
Enjoy!

Calories | Protein | Fat | Carbs | Fiber | Sodium |
Calories	Protein	Fat	Carbs	Fiber	Sodium
334	15.2g	13.1g	8.5g	8.5g	224mg

Vegetables Piadina

Cooking Time | Serving

11 min   4

2 zucchinis, ends removed, thinly sliced lengthwise
1 teaspoon dried oregano
1/2 teaspoon freshly ground black pepper
1/2 teaspoon garlic powder
1/2 cup hummus
4 whole wheat tortillas
4 Roma tomatoes, cut lengthwise into slices
2 cups chopped kale
4 tablespoons chopped red onion
1 teaspoon ground cumin

Slice the zucchini
Put them in a pan over medium heat and cook each side for 3 minutes.
Add pepper and sprinkle with oregano and garlic powder.
In a pan over medium heat, add the zucchini slices and cook for 3 minutes per side. Sprinkle with the oregano, pepper, and garlic powder and remove from the heat.
Spread 2 tablespoons of hummus on each tortilla. Lay the zucchini in the center of each.
Add tomato, kale, red onion, and cumin.
Wrap tightly and serve.
Enjoy!

Calories	Protein	Fat	Carbs	Fiber	Sodium
243	8.3g	8.2g	34.2g	7.4g	334

Vegan Bowls

Cooking Time | Serving

10 min   2

- 1 ½ cups whole-wheat orzo, cooked
- 7 ounces canned cannellini beans, drained and rinsed
- 1/2 yellow bell pepper, cubed
- 1/2 green bell pepper, cubed
- A pinch of salt and black pepper
- 1 and 1/2 tomatoes, cubed
- 1/2 red onion, chopped
- 1/2 cup mint, chopped
- 1 cups feta cheese, crumbled
- 1 tablespoon olive oil
- 1/8 cup lemon juice
- 1/2 tablespoon lemon zest, grated
- 1/2 cucumber, cubed
- 1 cup kalamata olives, pitted and sliced
- 1 and 1/2 garlic cloves, minced

In a large bowl, combine all the ingredients, toss, divide the mix between plates and serve
Enjoy

Calories	Protein	Fat	Carbs	Fiber
412	17	16	14	52

Herbed Chicken Pas

Cooking Time | Serving
30 min   2

- 1 ½ **thick chicken sausages, removed from casing and crumbled**
- **1/2 medium shallot, chopped**
- **1 cup diced baby portobello mushrooms**
- **1/2 teaspoon garlic powder**
- **1/2 tablespoon extra-virgin olive oil**
- **1/2 pound bean-based penne pasta**
- **2 medium Roma tomatoes, chopped**
- **1/2 (14.5-ounce) can of crushed tomatoes**
- 1 ½ **tablespoon heavy cream**

Place a large pan over medium-high heat. Add some oil and the sausage to the pan for 5 minutes, mixing breaking the sausage up until it is halfway cooked.
Reduce the heat to medium-low and put the shallot in Let it cook for 3 more minutes.
Put the mushrooms, add some garlic powder and olive oil and cook for 6 minutes, until all the water is co out.
In the meantime, bring a large pot of water to a boil add a handful of salt.
Cook the pasta in the boiling water for half of the co time, then drain the pasta keeping its water.
To the skillet, add the chopped and canned tomatoe cook for 4 minutes until the liquid thickens slightly.
Toss the pasta into the pan together with all the ingre and a full ladle of pasta water
Mix well until the water drains, then add more pasta v
Repeat this for the remaining pasta cooking time or u is al dente.
Reduce the heat and add the cream; mix well.

Calories | Protein | Fat | Car
706   45g   31g   79g

Mushrooms Risotto

Cooking Time | Serving
35 min   4

- Risotto
- 4 tablespoon. olive oil
- 2 onions, very finely chopped
- 26 oz. Arborio rice
- 8 cups sliced mushrooms (porcini or champignon)
- 1 cup dry white wine
- 2 Tablespoon. thyme leaves, finely chopped
- 6 Tablespoon. butter
- 1 cup grated parmesan cheese
- Salt and pepper
- Stock
- 1 Onion
- 1 Carrot
- 1 Potato
- 1 Celery stalk
- 4 thyme leaves
- Salt and pepper

Stock
Fill a pot with 15 cups of water
put all the stock ingredients in water
Place on medium heat for 40 minutes

Risotto
Put the onion in the pan over medium heat with the olive oil and let sauté until translucent.
Add mushrooms and cook for 5 minutes.
Put the rice in a pan and let it toast over medium heat; stir it regularly until it's hot and you can't handle it.
Add thyme leaves
Pour the cup of white wine and let it dry.
Start pouring three cups of stock into the pot and let the rice cook for 13 minutes, adding more stock when it gets dry; repeat the process of adding stock and stirring until dry.
After 13 minutes, remove from the heat and add butter, parmesan, salt, and pepper. Stir until the butter is completely melted.
Let it rest for 5 minutes (this is crucial)
Serve by pouring the rice on a plate and letting it disperse.
Enjoy!

Calories | Protein | Fat | Carbs |
604   26.2g   15.4g   82.3g

ntil Soup

Cooking Time | Serving

1 hour　　　　　　　4

¼ cup olive oil
1 white onion, chopped
3 carrots, chopped
3 cloves of garlic, minced
1 teaspoon cumin
1 teaspoon curry powder
½ teaspoon dried thyme
1 large can of diced tomatoes
1 cup of rinsed lentils
3 cups vegetable broth
2 cups water
1 pinch of salt
Ground black pepper to taste

In order to make a very good lentil soup, take a pot and start by heating some olive oil.

As soon as the oil begins to sizzle, add the chopped onion and carrot and cook, occasionally stirring, until the onion has softened and begins to turn translucent. This should take about 6 to 7 minutes.

Now add the spices. Stir continuously for about 30 seconds. Pour in the drained diced tomatoes and cook for a few more minutes, often stirring, to bring out the flavor.

Now add the lentils, broth, and water. Add 1 teaspoon salt and a pinch of pepper.

Now raise the heat and bring everything to a boil, then partially cover the pot and reduce the heat to maintain a gentle simmer.

Cook for 25-30 minutes, or until the lentils are tender but hold their shape.

Don't forget to add the chopped vegetables and cook for another 5 minutes, or until the vegetables have softened to your liking. Remove the pot from the heat and serve while still hot.

alories | Protein | Fat | Carbs | Fiber |

310　　　　19g　　　6.1g　　　46g　　　17.7g

Mustard Lentil Pate

Cooking Time | Serving

15 min　　　　　　　4

- 3/2 cup boiled lentils (or in the jar, well rinsed)
- The juice of half a lemon
- Salt
- Extra virgin olive oil
- 1 tablespoon of mustard
- A sprig of chopped parsley

Drain the lentils from the cooking water or the preserving liquid (if canned), wash them under water and blend them with the other ingredients.

Combine the chopped parsley.

Lentil Flour and Zucchini Crep

Cooking Time | Serving

5 min   2

- Lentil flour 4 tablespoons
- Spelled flour 2 tablespoons
- Oatmeal 1 tablespoon
- Zucchini 2
- Sparkling water to taste
- Olive oil e.v

In a bowl, pour flours, a pinch of salt, and
mix, adding water until you get a very f
batter.

Mix in boiled and mashed zucchini and p
over a thick-bottomed pan that is already
let it cook by turning it once.

Calories	Protein	Fat	Carbs	Fiber	cholester
158	7g	2g	2g	4g	9g

Spaghetti with Fennel Pesto and Hazelnuts

Cooking Time | Serving

15 min   4

- Whole wheat spaghetti 1 1/2 cups
- Fennel 1
- Garlic 2 cloves
- Hazelnuts with skin 3 tablespoons
- Water
- The grated lemon zest in a pinch
- 1 tablespoon lemon juice
- Salt and pepper to taste
- Olive oil, e.v. 4 tablespoons

Thinly slice the fennel with a mandoline and
sauté it for 5 minutes in a thick-bottomed pan
with the garlic and a tablespoon of oil.
Season with salt a little, lower the heat, and
cook covered for 5 minutes.
Meanwhile, toast the hazelnuts with a pinch of
salt and chop them in a blender.
When the fennel is cooked, blend it in an
immersion blender with the zest and juice
of the lemon, three tablespoons of oil, and a
few tablespoons of water needed to obtain a
smooth, velvety cream.
Boil the pasta al dente in lightly salted water.
Season with the sauce, serve on a plate and
sprinkle with the hazelnuts and add freshly
ground pepper.

Calories	Protein	Fat	Carbs	Fiber	Cholesterol	
158	10g	3.0g	22.10g	4.13g	12.23mg	

Cauliflower Pizzas

Cooking Time | Serving

25 min   3

Cauliflower florets 400g
Semintegral flour (type2) 70g
Cream of tartar 1 teaspoon
Salt half a teaspoon
Olive oil, e.v. 1 tablespoon + more for seasoning
Thick tomato puree q.b.
Oregano

Blend the cauliflower florets, flour, the cream of tartar, salt, and oil until a workable dough is obtained (it will be rather moist).

Shape into small balls the size of a tangerine and arrange them on a sheet of baking paper well spaced out; add another sheet of baking paper and roll them out with a rolling pin until to the thickness of 1.5 cm.

Place them in a baking dish with only the bottom sheet of paper and bake them for 35 min at 180 degrees (static).

After this time, sprinkle them with lightly salted tomato sauce and sprinkle with

Oregano. Bake for another 15 min about.

Wait for the pizzettas to cool and serve them with a drizzle of oil and more oregano.

Calories	Protein	Fat	Carbs	Fiber	Cholesterol
45	7.2g	3g	6.3g	2.4g	9.2g

Vegetarian Roast

Cooking Time | Serving

40 min   8

- 2 bunch beets, peeled and cut into 1-inch cubes
- 4 small sweet potatoes, peeled and cut into 1-inch cubes
- 6 parsnips, peeled and cut into 1-inch rounds
- 8 carrots, peeled and cut into 1-inch rounds
- 1 tablespoon raw honey
- 2 teaspoon sea salt
- 1 teaspoon freshly ground black pepper
- 2 tablespoon extra-virgin olive oil
- 4 tablespoons coconut oil, melted

Preheat the oven to 400ºF

Toss all the ingredients in a large bowl.

Carefully arrange the mixture on a baking sheet, then place it in the oven.

Let it cook for 25 minutes. Flip the vegetables after 12 minutes.

Let it cool and serve

Enjoy

Calories	Protein	Fat	Carbs	Fiber	Sodium
461	5.9g	18.1g	74.2g	14.0g	759mg

Cabbage and Olives Sautéed Sala

Cooking Time | Serving

20 min   4

- 2 bunch kale, leaves chopped and stems minced
- 1 cup celery leaves, roughly chopped, or additional parsley
- 1 bunch flat-leaf parsley, stems and leaves roughly chopped
- 4 garlic cloves, chopped
- 4 teaspoons olive oil
- 1/2 cup pitted Kalamata olives, chopped
- Grated zest and juice of 2 lemons
- Salt and pepper to taste

Set over a medium saucepan in a stea basket, and place the kale, celery lea parsley, and garlic.

Steam over medium-high heat for 15 min keeping it covered.

Once ready, squeeze out any excess liquid.

Place a pan with oil over medium heat.

Add the kale mixture to the pan, stirring, minutes.

Turn off the heat, and add the olives, ler zest, and juice.

Season with salt and pepper at the taste serve.

Enjoy

Calories | Protein | Fat | Carbs | Fiber | Sodiu

Calories	Protein	Fat	Carbs	Fiber	Sodium
84	2.2g	6.2g	7.2g	2.2g	273m

Brussels Sprouts and Boema Pumpkin Squash

Cooking Time | Serving

40 min   5

- 1 pound (455 g) Brussels sprouts, ends trimmed and outer leaves removed
- 2 medium boema squash, halved lengthwise, seeded, and cut into 1-inch pieces
- 2 cups fresh cranberries
- 4 teaspoons olive oil
- Salt and freshly ground black pepper to taste
- 1 cup balsamic vinegar
- 4 tablespoons roasted pumpkin seeds
- 4 tablespoons fresh pomegranate arils (seeds)

Preheat the oven to 400ºF.

Pick a bowl and put the Brussels sprouts, squash, and cranberries inside to mix them well.

Season with olive oil, salt, and pepper.

Toss well and arrange in a single layer on a sheet pan.

Cook in the oven for 30 minutes; remember to turn the vegetables halfway through the roasting time.

Meanwhile, simmer the vinegar for 10 to 12 minutes until the mixture becomes syrupy to make the balsamic glaze.

Once ready, drizzle the vegetables with balsamic syrup

Mix with pumpkin seeds and pomegranate arils.

Enjoy

Calories | Protein | Fat | Carbs | Fiber | Sodium |

Calories	Protein	Fat	Carbs	Fiber	Sodium
202	6.4g	6.6g	23g	8.5g	34mg

erb Seasoned White Beans

Cooking Time | Serving

22 min   4

2 tablespoon olive oil
4 garlic cloves, minced
2 (30-ounce) cans white cannellini beans, drained and rinsed
2 teaspoon minced fresh rosemary plus 1 whole fresh rosemary sprig
1/2 teaspoon dried sage
1 cup low-sodium chicken stock
Salt, to taste

Sautée the garlic in olive oil in a medium pan over low heat for 2 minutes

Mince the rosemary and mix with whole sprigs and sage leaves

Pour this mixture into the pan, then add the beans.

After 1 minute, pour the chicken stock into the pan and bring everything to a boil.

Reduce the heat to medium and let it cook until most of the liquid is evaporated. Meanwhile, smash some of the beans with a fork.

Remove the rosemary sprig.

Season with salt to taste

Serve and enjoy

alories | Protein | Fat | Carbs | Fiber | Sodium |

Calories	Protein	Fat	Carbs	Fiber	Sodium
152	6.2g	7.4g	17.5g	8.1g	154mg

Carrots with Orange and Honey Glaze

Cooking Time | Serving

30 min   4

- 1 pound of carrots, peeled
- 4 tablespoons fresh orange juice
- 2 tablespoon honey
- 1 teaspoon coriander
- Pinch salt

Prepare the oven to 400°F

Cut the carrots into julienne strips and put them in a bowl.

Mix the orange juice, honey, coriander, and salt in a different bowl.

Pour the mixture you just made over the carrots and mix to coat.

Spread the carrots in a baking dish, ensuring they are all on a single layer.

Roast until fork-tender (15 minutes).

Let's sit for 5 minutes

Serve and enjoy!

Calories | Protein | Fat | Carbs | Fiber | Sodium |

Calories	Protein	Fat	Carbs	Fiber	Sodium
83	1.2g	0.3g	23.0g	3.2g	146

Fish & Seafood

Salmon Cooked Icon Rosemary and Walnuts

Cooking Time | Serving

21 min   3 ounce

- 2 tablespoons of mustard
- 1 clove of garlic, finely chopped
- ¼ teaspoon freshly grated lemon zest
- 1 teaspoon freshly squeezed lemon juice
- 1 teaspoon chopped rosemary
- ½ teaspoon honey
- ½ teaspoon of salt
- ¼ teaspoon pepper
- 3 tablespoons breadcrumbs
- 3 tablespoons freshly chopped walnuts
- 1 teaspoon extra virgin olive oil
- 1 (1 pound) fresh skinless salmon fillet
- Olive oil to taste

In order to prepare this amazing salmon fillet with walnuts and rosemary, preheat the oven to 430 degrees F°. Line a baking sheet with baking paper.

In a bowl, mix mustard, garlic, lemon zest, lemon juice, honey, pepper, salt, and rosemary. Then take another bowl and add the walnuts and oil.

Lay the salmon on the baking sheet, spread the mixture over the salmon, and adhere the mixture to the salmon flesh as best you can.

Cook until the fish is cut in half by lightly placing a fork over it.

Before serving, sprinkle with fresh rosemary and lemon wedges as garnish.

Calories	Protein	Fat	Carbs	Sodium	Cholesterol
230	27g	14g	6g	270mg	70mg

icy Roasted Salmon with Cranberries

Cooking Time | Serving

30 min   8-9

2 ½ pounds of skinless salmon fillet
2 cloves of garlic, finely chopped
1 ½ teaspoons salt
½ teaspoon finely ground black pepper
1 lemon diced
2 ½ tablespoons extra virgin olive oil
2 and ½ teaspoons mustard
2 and ½ cups cranberries, fresh or frozen
1 shallot
1 seedless yellow bell pepper, chopped
1 apple, peeled and diced
1 celery stalk, thinly diced [ ]
1 and ½ tablespoons balsamic vinegar
2 tablespoons chopped fresh parsley

In order to prepare a fantastic salmon roast, preheat the oven to 400 degrees F°.

Line a baking sheet with the baking paper provided. As soon as the oven is ready, arrange the salmon on the baking sheet. Separately, combine the garlic, salt, pepper, and lemon zest and mix everything well.

Then spread over the salmon and place in the oven.

Simultaneously chop the cranberries, shallots, and serrano in a food processor until finely chopped. Transfer to a medium basin and toss with the apple, celery, vinegar, 1 tablespoon parsley, and the remaining tablespoon oil and 1/2 teaspoon salt.

Now sprinkle the salmon with the remaining mixture. Add the parsley and serve.

Calories	Protein	Fat	Carbs	Fiber	Sugar	Cholesterol
234	29g	9g	8.1g	1.9g	5.1g	66.5g

Miso with Salmon

Cooking Time | Serving

15 min   8-9

- 2 lemons
- 2 limes
- ¼ cup of white miso
- 2 tablespoons of extra virgin olive oil
- 2½ tablespoons maple syrup
- ¼ teaspoon ground pepper
- Pinch of cayenne pepper
- 1 skinless salmon fillet
- Sliced shallots for garnish

To prepare a fantastic miso dish with salmon, place the rack in the top third of the oven; preheat the grill to cook your salmon at a high temperature. Line a large baking sheet with aluminum foil.

Separately, squeeze 1 lemon and 1 lime into a small bowl. Add the miso, oil, maple syrup, pepper, and cayenne. Place the salmon side down on the baking sheet and spread the miso mixture on top. Then lay the remaining lemon and lime and place them on the sides of the salmon, cut sides up.

Cook the salmon until it becomes very tender, about 10 to 12 minutes. Serve with the lime and lemon on the side, shallots, and a pinch of coarse salt.

Calories	Protein	Fat	Carbs	Fiber	Sugar	Cholester-
247	30g	9g	7g	0.1g	3.5g	71mg

Salmon in Gre

Cooking Time | Serving

40 min   2

- 2 tablespoons extra-virgin olive oil, divided
- 1/2 tablespoon smoked paprika
- 1/4 teaspoon salt, divided, plus a pinch
- 1/2 (7 ounces) can no-salt-added chickpeas, rinsed
- 1/6 cup buttermilk
- 1/8 cup mayonnaise
- 1/8 cup chopped fresh chives and/or dill, plus more for garnish
- 1/4 teaspoon ground pepper, divided
- 1/8 teaspoon garlic powder
- 5 cups chopped kale
- 1/8 cup water
- 1 pound wild salmon, cut into 4 portions

Preheat your oven to 425F; Position racks in upper third and middle.

Very thoroughly pat chickpeas dry, then toss a mixture of 1 tablespoon oil, paprika, and teaspoon salt. Bake the chickpeas on a baking s on the upper rack for 25 minutes, stirring three through baking time.

In a blender, mix buttermilk, mayonnaise, h pepper, and garlic powder until smooth, and set aside.

Cook kale for 2 minutes in a large pot with oliv occasionally stirring. Keep cooking, adding a 1/2 of water every time it gets dry until the kale is te Remove from heat, add salt, and stir.

When the chickpeas are ready, push them to one of the pan. Put salmon on the other side and se with the remaining salt and pepper. Bake again salmon is cooked through.

Pour the dressing on the salmon, add a little herbs to taste, and serve together with the kale chickpeas.

Calories	Protein	Fat	Carbs	Fiber	Sodium	Choleste
443	32g	21.3	23.6g	6.3g	556.7	72.9

Bruxelles Roasted Salmon

Cooking Time | Serving

45 min   3

- 7 large cloves of garlic, divided
- 1/2 cup extra-virgin olive oil
- 1 tablespoon finely chopped fresh oregano, divided
- 1/2 teaspoon salt, divided
- 1/3 teaspoon freshly ground pepper, divided
- 3 cups Brussels sprouts, trimmed and sliced
- 1/3 cup white wine, preferably Chardonnay
- 1 pound wild-caught salmon fillet, skinned, cut into 3 portions
- Lemon wedges

Position the racks in the middle of the oven and preheat them to 450 degrees F.

In a medium-sized bowl, mix 1 tbsp of oregano, 1/2 tbsp salt, and 1/2 tbsp pepper with 2 minced garlic cloves.

In a big roasting pan, toss the Bruxelles sprouts with the remaining garlic in 3 tbsp of seasoned oil.

Stir and roast in the oven for 15 minutes.

Remove the pan from the oven, stir the vegetables and place salmon on top. Pour the white wine and sprinkle with the remaining oregano, salt, and pepper.

Bake for 5 to 10 minutes more until the salmon is cooked through. Serve with lemon wedges.

Calories	Protein	Fat	Carbs	Fiber	Sodium	Cholesterol
344	32.1g	15.2g	12.3g	2.3g	485mg	70.2

agna Cauda Green Salmon

Cooking Time | Serving

40 min   8

2-pound fingerling potatoes, halved if large, and/or sweet potato, cut into 1/2- inch-thick wedges
2 bunch broccolini, trimmed
2 tablespoon extra-virgin olive oil
1 teaspoon salt, divided
2-pound salmon (see Tips)
2 small fennel bulbs, cut into 1/2-inch-thick wedges, fronds reserved
4 medium heads Belgian endive, leaves separated
1 small head radicchio, cut into 1/2-inch-thick wedges
Bagna Cauda
1 cup extra-virgin olive oil
4 cloves garlic, very thinly sliced
16 anchovy fillets
4 tablespoons sherry vinegar
2 tablespoon butter

Roasted Salmon
Preheat the oven to 425 degrees F.
Prepare a baking sheet covered with cooking spray.
Mix potatoes, broccolini, 1 tbsp oil, and 1/2 tbsp salt in a bowl and toss them. Transfer only potatoes to the baking sheet and roast them for 15 minutes, turning them once halfway.
Place the salmon in the center of the baking sheets, pushing the potatoes to the edges. Then arrange the broccoli right around the salmon and sprinkle the remaining salt on it.
Roast for about 8 minutes, and in the meantime, prepare the bagna cauda.

Bagna Cauda
Sautée the garlic in a small pan with olive oil over low heat for 2 minutes.
Add anchovies, vinegar, and butter and often stir, letting the anchovies flake apart. Keep cooking over very low heat for 2 minutes.
Carefully set the roasted salmon and vegetables with fennel, endive, and radicchio on a platter.
Drizzle with bagna cauda or let it aside for dipping

ories	Protein	Fat	Carbs	Fiber	Sodium	Cholesterol	Calcium
533	31.2gg	30.3g	35.4g	5g	7059.6mg	67.5mg	133.2mg

Sunrise Salmon

Cooking Time | Serving

30 min   4

- Fresh salmon fillet
- Seasoning:
- 1 tbsp di cumin,
- 1 tbsp paprika,
- 1 tbsp pepper,
- 1 tbsp Cayenne pepper,
- 1 tbsp black pepper,
- Garlic and onion at the taste

Prepare the pan by putting it on high heat for 2 minutes.

In the meantime, mix all the ingredients for seasoning and pour the mixture on the salmon. Don't put it on the skin side.

Turn down the heat to medium-high.

Gently put the salmon in the pan, keeping the seasoned side face down for 6 minutes.

Turn down the heat again to medium-low and turn the salmon face up.

Keep cooking for 6 more minutes.

Serve and enjoy

Calories | Protein | Fat | Carbs | Sugar |

193   27.3g   8.2g   0.5g   0.1g

Zucchini Noodles with King Prau

Cooking Time | Serving

5-15 min   2

- 2 tablespoons butter
- 4 teaspoons olive oil
- 4 cloves of garlic, minced
- 1 kg raw, shelled, and peeled prawns
- 2 teaspoons crushed red pepper
- 120 g of chicken broth
- 2 tablespoons lemon juice
- 1 teaspoon lemon zest
- 1/2 teaspoon salt
- 6 small spiral zucchini

Melt butter in a skillet and add olive oil.

Add the garlic, shrimp, and ground red pe di.

Cook for about 4 minutes, stirring occasion

When the shrimp are pink, add the chi broth, juice, and lemon zest.

Sprinkle with salt. Bring to a boil.

Add zucchini noodles and stir to mix everyt together, about 1 to 2

minutes. Serve hot.

Avocado Gremolata Salmon

Cooking Time | Serving

10 min   6

- 6 Salmon fillets (two 4-5 ounces each) or two larger 10-ounce salmon fillets with skin
- 3-4 tbsp olive oil, avocado oil, or butter for pan
- Kosher salt and black pepper, to taste
- Avocado Gremolata
- 1 small avocado (ripe) diced
- 4 tsp dried parsley or 1/3 c fresh chopped
- 2 garlic cloves -minced
- 1/4 tsp Lemon pepper seasoning or peppercorns
- 1/4 tsp Sea Salt
- 3–4 tbsp extra virgin olive oil
- lemon juice 1 of one lemon and slices to garnish

To Make the avocado gremolata
Peel the Avocado and chop it
mix the Avocado with herbs
Mix all the ingredients together in a small bowl and put it in the fridge for 15 minutes

To make salmon:
Firstly take your salmon and wash it under cold water and pat it dry.
Add butter to a large hot pan and let it melt completely.
Put the salmon in the pan, and keep cooking with the flesh face down for 3 minutes. Then flip it with a spatula, placing the skin down.
Use the spatula to press down on the flesh, sealing the skin against the pan to create super crispy skin.
After 4 minutes, the salmon is ready. (Check the inside to be sure it's no longer pink or opaque)
Turn off the heat and let the salmon sit for 5 minutes. It should continue cooking off the heat.
Top with salt, pepper, lemon, and Avocado gremolata.

Calories	Protein	Fat	Carbs	Fiber	Sodium	Cholesterol
364	22.3g	29.4g	5.4g	3.4g	274.3mg	48.5g

allops with Fresh Tomatoes

Cooking Time | Serving

30 min   4

Fresh sea scallops 0.9 kg
4 teaspoons of olive oil
1 teaspoon salt and pepper
Diced tomatoes 3 cups
Fresh lime juice - 2 tablespoons
1 shallot sliced
fresh cilantro to taste

Dry scallops with paper towels and season with pepper and salt.
Add oil to a skillet and heat over medium-high heat.
Add the scallops to the pan and cook on each side for about 2 minutes
Remove scallops and set them aside.
Add salt, pepper, shallots, cilantro, and tomatoes to the skillet.
Bring the mixture to a boil and scrape all brown bits from the bottom of the pan.
Once it starts to boil, lower the heat to medium and simmer for about 10 minutes.
Return the scallops to the pan and cook for another 5 minutes. Plate and serve immediately

lories	Protein	Fat	Carbs	Fiber	Sugar
258	36g	6.4g	13.9g	3.5g	5.4g

Shrimp and Avocado Lettuce Strips

Cooking Time | Serving

21 min   8

- 2kg g raw shrimp, shelled and hulled
- 8 teaspoons olive oil, divided
- 340 g avocado
- 2 cups plain Greek yogurt
- 4 tablespoons lime juice, divided
- 720 g diced tomato
- 120 g diced green bell pepper
- 120 g chopped cilantro
- 120 g chopped red onion
- 24 large romaine lettuce leaves

Place shrimp and dressing in a large bowl and mix vigorously.

Heat 2 teaspoons of olive oil in a skillet and add the seasoned shrimp

Cook for 5 minutes on both sides until shrimp are pink and cooked through.

Combine the Avocado, Greek yogurt, and 1 tablespoon of lime juice in a food processor and process the mixture until it becomes completely liquid.

Take a bowl and mix inside the jalapeno bell pepper, tomatoes, onion, cilantro, and lime juice, making sure to stir carefully to create a smooth mixture.

Plate by carefully placing the shrimp between the lettuce leaves, and add the avocado mixture and tomato mixture.

Serve immediately.

Seafood Stuffed Pasta She

Cooking Time | Serving

55 min   4

- 1 cup butter
- 1 cup chopped green pepper
- 1 cup chopped onion
- 1 cup chopped celery
- Drained and flaky crabmeat
- 1 pound of medium-sized shrimp - peeled and deveined
- 1 cup spiced and seasoned breadcrumbs
- 2 can of mushroom cream (10.75 ounces) condensed chicken broth
- 200g of pasta shells

Filling
Preheat the oven to 350F.

In a large pan, put the butter over medium heat and melt before adding pepper, onion, celery, crabmea shrimps. Stir the mixture for about 5 minutes, be caref to let it stick to the pan.

Add breadcrumbs and stir the vegetables and seafo the pan.

Add all of the mushroom cream and chicken broth to
Coat a baking dish with butter and pour the mixture
Bake in the oven until lightly roasted (at least 25 minu

Pasta
Put a pot full of cold water on high heat and bring it t
Once boiling, add 2 tbsp of salt
put the pasta into the water and let it cook for 12 m (try it to make sure it is cooked)
Remove water and fill every pasta shell with the m you made before
Serve and enjoy

Calories | Protein | Fat | Carbs | Sodium | Cholester

Calories	Protein	Fat	Carbs	Sodium	Cholester
342	17g	15.4g	28.5g	1142mg	95mg

Salmon Balls

Cooking Time | Serving

30 min 4

- 4 cans of salmon, drained and crumbled
- 3/2 cup Italian breadcrumbs
- 1 cup chopped fresh parsley
- 4 eggs, beaten
- 4 green onions, minced
- 4 teaspoons of seafood herbs
- 3 teaspoon ground black pepper
- 3 teaspoons garlic powder
- 6 tablespoons Worcestershire sauce
- 4 tablespoons Dijon mustard
- 6 tablespoons grated Parmesan
- 4 tablespoons creamy vinaigrette
- 2 tablespoon olive oil

Pick a big bowl and put all the ingredients in it; energetically mix them using your hands until it becomes a uniform mixture. Then divide the mixture, shape it into 16 balls, and then smash them to create disk-shaped patties.

Heat olive oil in a frying pan on medium heat. Cook the salmon balls until golden brown, 5 to 7 minutes per side until golden brown

Serve them and enjoy!

Calories | Protein | Fat | Carbs | Sodium | Cholesterol |

Calories	Protein	Fat	Carbs	Sodium	Cholesterol
262	27.2g	12.5g	10.4g	783mg	96mg

Gourmet Tuna Patties

Cooking Time | Serving

30 min 4

- 4 teaspoons lemon juice
- 6 tablespoons grated Parmesan
- 4 eggs
- 20 tablespoons Italian breadcrumbs
- 6 tuna cans, drained
- 6 tablespoons diced onion
- 2 pinch of ground black pepper
- 3 tablespoons vegetable oil

Pick a big bowl and beat lemon juice and eggs in it.

In the same bowl, add cheese and breadcrumbs, and mix them until you obtain a paste.

Add tuna and chopped onion and keep mixing until you get a smooth mixture, season with black pepper.

Use the mixture to form 1-inch thick patties.

Heat the vegetable oil in a pan over low heat; use as less as possible, just the necessary to prevent food from sticking; cook the patties until golden brown.

Calories | Protein | Fat | Carbs | Sodium | Cholesterol |

Calories	Protein	Fat	Carbs	Sodium	Cholesterol
323	31.5g	15.4g	13.4g	409mg	124mg

Shrimp Cocktail Tramezzini

Cooking Time | Serving

15 min   4

- 3 cups cheddar, shredded
- 12 ounces canned tiny shrimp, drained
- 6 tablespoons yogurt mayonnaise (or chickpeas hummus)
- 3 tablespoons green onions, chopped
- 8 whole-wheat bread slices

In a bowl, put shrimp with cheese, green onion, and yogurt mayo to properly mix them into
Fill your sandwiches with the shrimp mixture and cut them in half diagonally
Place sandwiches in the oven and cook at 350 F for 5 minutes.
Let sandwiches cool for 2 minutes
Enjoy!

Calories | Protein | Fat | Carbs | Fiber |

Calories	Protein	Fat	Carbs	Fiber
163	5g	2g	14g	4g

Garlic Scented Shrimps with Creamy Mushrooms S

Cooking Time | Serving

25 min   2

- 1/2 pound (225 g) fresh shrimp, peeled, deveined, and patted dry
- 1/2 teaspoon salt
- 1/2 cup extra-virgin olive oil
- 4 large garlic cloves, thinly sliced
- 2 ounces (60 g) sliced mushrooms (shiitake, baby bella, or button)
- 1/4 teaspoon red pepper flakes
- 1/8 cup chopped fresh flat-leaf Italian parsley

Season the shrimp with salt and set them a in a medium bowl
Put the olive oil in a large pan over low hea
Add the garlic and let it sauté for 4 min until fragrant; occasionally stir.
Insert the mushrooms into the pan and them cook until they release their juice
Add shrimps to the pan and cook for 4 min then sprinkle with red pepper flakes.
Turn off the heat and add parsley
Stir and serve warm.

Calories | Protein | Fat | Carbs | Fiber | Sodiu

Calories	Protein	Fat	Carbs	Fiber	Sodiu
614	24.4g	55.3g	3.2g	0	734

Sweet Sour Salmon

Cooking Time | Serving

25 min   2

- 1 tablespoon whole-grain mustard
- 1 garlic clove, minced
- 1/2 tablespoon honey
- 1/8 teaspoon salt
- 1/8 teaspoon freshly ground black pepper
- 1/2 pound salmon fillet
- Nonstick cooking spray

Prepare the oven, heating it to 425F. Coat a baking sheet with nonstick cooking spray (or greaseproof paper).

Pick a small bowl to make the sauce, then use it to stir together the mustard, garlic, honey, salt, and pepper

Coat the salmon fillet with the mustard mixture and then lean it on the baking sheet, skin face down

Cook in the oven for 15 to 20 minutes (it should flake apart easily)

Serve hot and enjoy.

Calories | Protein | Fat | Carbs | Fiber | Sodium |

Calories	Protein	Fat	Carbs	Fiber	Sodium
184	23.6g	7.5g	5.3g	0	316

...oked Salmon on Cucumber Rounds

Cooking Time | Serving

70-130 min   10

225 g softened light cream cheese
¼ cup (15 g) finely chopped parsley
225 g finely chopped smoked salmon
1 teaspoon lemon zest
¼ cup (58 g) low-fat sour cream
2 cucumbers.

In a medium-sized bowl, mix all the ingredients except the cucumbers mix Welland, and refrigerate for 2 hours to chill. Peel and slice the cucumbers and place them in rounds on a paper towel to dry slightly on one side; arrange the cucumber rounds on a serving plate, and place a small amount of salmon mixture on the dry side of each cucumber round (about ½ teaspoon).

...lories | Protein | Fat | Carbs | Fiber | Sodium | Cholesterol |

Calories	Protein	Fat	Carbs	Fiber	Sodium	Cholesterol
110	5g	6g	1g	1g	283	19mg

Scallops

Cooking Time | Serving
21 min   2-3

- 6 scallops
- 1 cup of lemon juice
- 1 tuft of parsley
- 1 clove of garlic
- Olive oil to taste.
- Salt and pepper to taste

Open the scallops. Do this using a knife to force between the two shells, then peel them off the shell, and remove the stringy part and the dark part using kitchen scissors. Wash them well under fresh running water very carefully because there are often sand residues. After removing them from the shell, massage the scallops with salt and pepper to season. Having done this, heat a frying pan with a little oil and add the garlic. Fry the garlic briefly and add the scallops for about a minute and a half on each side. Add the lemon juice and let it evaporate.
Wash and chop the fresh parsley in the meantime. Finish cooking the scallops and adding the chopped fresh parsley. Serve the scallops cooked and still hot.

Calories | Protein | Fat | Carbs |
135   12g   6g   1g

Crab So

Cooking Time | Serving
80 min   6

- Two 390 g cans of vegetable stock
- 1 cup (235 ml) tomato sauce
- 1 medium onion, diced
- 2 finely diced stalks of celery
- 1 tablespoon (4 g) finely chopped fresh thyme
- 1 bay leaf
- 2 tablespoons (18 g) of seafood seasoning
- ½ cup (92 g) barley
- 455 g crab meat pieces
- 2 cups (140 g) grated green cabbage
- 2 diced carrots
- 1 large diced potato
- salt and pepper to taste.

Put the first 9 ingredients in a large pot, b to a boil, lower the heat and simmer fo minutes on low heat. Add the vegetables cook for a further 25 minutes until the pota are tender.

Calories | Protein | Fat | Carbs | Fiber | Cholester
233   22g   2.5g   30g   6g   65

Grilled Catfish Sandwich

Cooking Time | Serving

20 min   4

- 4 x 160 g catfish fillets
- ¼ cup (32 g) cornflour
- 1 teaspoon cumin
- 1 teaspoon salt
- ½ teaspoon cayenne pepper optional
- 2 egg whites whipped to stiff peaks
- canola oil spray
- 3 whole-wheat sandwiches
- 4 to 8 red leaf lettuce leaves
- 1 sliced tomato
- mustard to taste.

Rinse the catfish fillets and dry them with paper towels. Put the cornflour, cumin, salt, and cayenne pepper on a soup plate and mix well; put the egg whites on a separate soup plate.

Rinse the catfish fillets first in the egg whites, then in the cornflour mixture, pressing in the cornflour to coat the fillets well.

Spray both sides of each fillet with canola oil spray. Grill the fillets for 3 to 4 minutes per side on a grill set at 392°F with the lid on. Serve with whole wheat rolls, lettuce, tomato, and mustard.

Calories	Protein	Fat	Carbs	Fiber	Cholesterol
482	40g	18g	26g	5g	100mg

Swordfish Carpaccio

Cooking Time | Serving

130 min   1

210 g swordfish cut into very thin slices
Juice half a lemon
22 ml olive oil
A sprig of parsley
Olive oil to taste
Ginger powder to taste
Salt and pepper to taste

Start by placing the swordfish slices in the freezer for at least two hours in order to eliminate possible bacteria. After two hours, take the swordfish out of the freezer.

Now arrange the swordfish slices broadly in an oven dish or baking tray.

Meanwhile, prepare the marinade. In a bowl, pour the olive oil, and add pepper, salt, and ginger powder. Mix all the ingredients well and now take care of the parsley. Wash it, dry it and chop it finely. Now also add the parsley to the marinade.

Pour the marinade into the baking dish where you have placed the swordfish slices and cover with transparent paper. Leave the carpaccio to marinate in the fridge for at least 7 hours. When it is time to serve the carpaccio, take the fish slices and arrange them on a plate without marinade, dress with a drizzle of raw olive oil and serve with a fresh salad.

Calories	Protein	Fat	Carbs
400	39g	30g	1g

Spaghetti with Smoked Salmon

Cooking Time | Serving

15 min   2

- 5/4 Semintegral or whole-grain spaghetti
- 1/2 cup smoked salmon
- The juice of half a lemon
- Olive oil, e.v. 2 tablespoons
- Parsley, salt, and pepper to taste.

Boil spaghetti in plenty of salted water
Meanwhile, in a bowl, marinate the chopped salmon with a mixture of oil, lemon parsley, and pepper.
When the cooking time is over, add the spaghetti, mixing carefully.
Serve hot and enjoy

Calories | Protein | Fat | Carbs | Fiber | Cholesterol |

Calories	Protein	Fat	Carbs	Fiber	Cholesterol
158	10.50g	3g	22.10g	4.10	11mg

Bronte's Baked Fi

Cooking Time | Serving

30 min   8

- 1 cup extra-virgin olive oil, divided
- 2 pound (900 g) flaky white fish (such as cod, haddock, or halibut), skin removed
- 1 cup shelled finely chopped pistachios
- 1 cup ground flaxseed
- Zest and juice of 2 lemons, divided
- 2 teaspoon ground cumin
- 2 teaspoon ground allspice
- 1 teaspoon salt
- 1/2 teaspoon freshly ground black pepper

Preheat the oven to 400ºF
Coat a baking sheet with 2 tbsp olive oil.
Split the fish in 4 and arrange it on the ba sheet
In a small bowl, mix all the nuts and seeds the lemon zest, cumin, salt, and pepper, toss well.
Spread the nut mixture on the fish, toge with the lemon juice and the remaining oil. Bake for 17 more minutes.
Let it sit outside the oven for 5 minutes
Serve and enjoy

Calories | Protein | Fat | Carbs | Fiber | Sodiu

Calories	Protein	Fat	Carbs	Fiber	Sodiu
503	26.4g	41.2g	9.5g	6.32g	334m

Fresh Salmon wraps

Cooking Time | Serving

10 min   3

- 1/2 pound (454 g) salmon fillets, cooked and flaked
- 1/4 cup diced carrots
- 1/4 cup diced celery
- 1 1/2 tablespoons diced red onion
- 1 1/2 tablespoons chopped fresh dill
- 1 tablespoons capers
- 2/3 tablespoons extra-virgin olive oil
- 1/2 tablespoon aged balsamic vinegar
- 1/8 teaspoon kosher or sea salt
- 1/4 teaspoon freshly ground black pepper
- 3 whole-wheat flatbread wraps or soft whole-wheat tortillas

Put all the ingredients, except for the wraps, in a big bowl and toss them well to create a fresh salad

Let the heat of the wrap on a pan medium heat for 1 minute on each side. In order to make them more flexible

Adapt the wraps on a clean surface and evenly divide the salmon mixture among the wraps. Fold up the bottom of the wraps, then roll up the wrap to seal it

Serve immediately.

Calories	Protein	Fat	Carbs	Fiber	Sodium
193	18.5g	8.2g	13.2	3.3g	531mg

na and Olive Salad Sandwiches

Cooking Time | Serving

10 min   8

6 tablespoons freshly squeezed lemon juice
4 tablespoons extra-virgin olive oil
2 garlic cloves, minced
1 teaspoon freshly ground black pepper
4 (5-ounce / 142-g) cans tuna, drained
2 (2.25-ounce / 64-g) can sliced olives, any green or black variety
1 cup chopped fresh fennel, including fronds
16 slices of whole-grain crusty bread

Use a medium bowl to mix the salad seasoning ingredients such as lemon juice, oil, garlic, and pepper.

Put tuna into a plate and separate it into chunks using a fork.

Add chunked tuna into the bowl, together with fennel and olives. Stir to incorporate all the ingredients.

Divide the tuna salad equally among 8 slices of bread. Top each with the remaining bread slices.

Let them sit for at least 5 minutes so the seasoning can soak into the bread and make it taste a lot better.

Serve and enjoy

lories	Protein	Fat	Carbs	Fiber	Sodium
952	165g	17g	37g	7g	2572mg

Grilled Salmon

Cooking Time | Serving

20 min   2

- 2 (4-ounce / 113-g) salmon fillets
- 1 1/2 tablespoons miso paste
- 1 tablespoon raw honey
- 1/2 teaspoon coconut aminos
- 1/2 teaspoon rice vinegar

Preheat the grill.

Lay the salmon filets on a baking dish with an aluminum foil

Whisk together the miso paste, honey, coconut aminos, and vinegar in a small bowl.

Pour miso paste, coconut aminos, honey, and vinegar in a bowl and energetically whisk them together.

Use a brush to evenly spread the glaze you just made on top of the salmon

Grill until the salmon is browned on top

Grill for 5 more minutes after brushing any remaining glaze.

Leave it for 5 minutes so it can cool,

serve and enjoy!

Calories | Protein | Fat | Carbs | Fiber | Sodium |

Calories	Protein	Fat	Carbs	Fiber	Sodium
262	30.3g	8.5g	12.5g	0.6g	716

Italian Grilled Shrin.

Cooking Time | Serving

25 min   2

- 1 tablespoon garlic, minced
- 1 tablespoon fresh Italian parsley, finely chopped
- ¼ cup extra-virgin olive oil
- ½ cup lemon juice
- 1/2 teaspoon salt
- 1 pound1 (450 g) jumbo shrimp (11 to 15), peeled and deveined
- Special Equipment:
- 2 wooden skewers, soaked in water for at least 30 minutes

In a big bowl, put the garlic, parsley, oliv lemon juice, and salt and whisk them toge

Add the ship to the bowl and toss to let it in the marinade

Let it sit aside for at least 15 minutes

Skewer the shrimps (max 4-5 per skewer)

Prepare the grill setting it to high heat.

Grill the skewer shrimps until pink (5 min and flip them halfway through

Serve hot and enjoy

Calories | Protein | Fat | Carbs | Fiber | Sodiu

Calories	Protein	Fat	Carbs	Fiber	Sodiu
405	56.4g	17.83g	3.93g	0.4g	1222m

Orzo Shrimp Salad

Cooking Time | Serving

32 min   2

- 1/2 cup orzo
- 1/2 hothouse cucumber, deseeded and chopped
- 1/4 cup finely diced red onion
- 1 tablespoon extra-virgin olive oil
- 1 pounds shrimps, peeled and deveined
- 1 1/2 lemons, juiced
- Salt and freshly ground black pepper to taste
- 1/2 cup crumbled feta cheese
- 1 tablespoon dried dill
- 1/2 cup chopped fresh flat-leaf parsley

Fill a large pot with water and bring it to a boil.
Add a bunch of salt, then orzo, and cook for 25 minutes.
Drain using a colander and set aside.
Heat olive oil in a pan over medium-low heat
Add shrimps and let them cook on both sides for 2 minutes.
Add the cooked shrimp to a big bowl, and combine with cucumber and red onion.
Add the orzo to the bowl, sprinkle with lemon juice and toss to combine.
Add salt, pepper, and feta cheese, and stir to properly combine the salad.
Garnish with the parsley and serve.

Calories	Protein	Fat	Carbs	Fiber	Sodium
565	63.3g	17.8g	43.9g	4.1g	2225mg

Marinated Shrimp Salad with Avocado

Cooking Time | Serving

15 min   2

1/2 pound fresh shrimp, peeled, deveined, and cut in half lengthwise
1/2 small red or yellow bell pepper, cut into ½-inch chunks
1/4 small red onion, cut into thin slivers
1/4 English cucumber, peeled and cut into ½-inch chunks
1/8 cup chopped fresh cilantro
1/4 cup extra-virgin olive oil
1/6 cup freshly squeezed lime juice
1 tablespoon freshly squeezed clementine juice
1 tablespoon freshly squeezed lemon juice
1/2 teaspoon salt
1/4 teaspoon freshly ground black pepper
1 ripe avocado,

Combine the shrimp, bell pepper, red onion, cucumber, and coriander in a bowl
Make a sauce to marinate the shrimps, stirring together olive oil, lime, clementine, lemon juice, salt, and black pepper. Keep stirring until smooth.
Coat the shrimps with the mixture you just made and cover the bowl using plastic wrap.
Transfer to the refrigerator to marinate for at least 2 hours or up to 8 hours.
Peel the avocado and cut it into 1/2-inch wide chunks
After marinating, add the avocado chunks into the mixture and toss them.
Serve and enjoy.

Calories	Protein	Fat	Carbs	Fiber	Sodium
494	24.3g	33.5g	13.5g	6.05g	752mg

Baked Salmon with a Taste of Lemon

Cooking Time | Serving

25 min   2

- 1/8 teaspoon dried thyme
- Zest and juice of ½ lemon
- 1/8 teaspoon salt
- 1/4 teaspoon freshly ground black pepper
- 1/2 pound (454 g) salmon fillet
- Nonstick cooking spray

Prepare the oven to 425 F. Pick a medium baking sheet and cover it with nonstick cooking spray (or greaseproof paper).

Pick a small bowl and combine together thyme, lemon zest and juice, salt, and pepper. Stir well to incorporate

Coat the salmon with the lemon-scented mixture, and spread it all over.

Arrange the salmon on the baking sheet facing the skin down

Bake the salmon for about 15 minutes, and taste it before removing it from the oven

Calories | Protein | Fat | Carbs | Fiber | Sodium |

163   23.5g   7.4g   1.2g   0   165mg

Poultry
Recipes

Greek Special Roasted Chick

Cooking Time | Serving

50 min   2

- 0.8 lbs bone-in chicken thighs with skin (approx. 5 –6 thighs)
- For the Greek dressing
- 1 sprig rosemary
- 1/8 cup olive oil, plus more for the pan
- 1/4 lemon, juiced
- 1 tbsp balsamic vinegar
- 1 1/2 garlic cloves (or 2 tsp minced)
- 1/4 tsp kosher or sea salt, plus add 'l pinch for seasoning chicken
- 1/4 tsp black pepper
- 1/2 tsp dried oregano
- 1 chopped shallots or 1 medium yellow onion, sliced
- 1/2 lemon, thinly sliced
- 1 tablespoon chopped fresh parsley (for garnish)

Pat chicken dry with paper towels, then set aside
Preheat oven to 400F
Roast rosemary in a dry pan for 3 minutes, leaves are fragrant and charred
Strip rosemary leaves and place in a medium b
Add olive oil, lemon juice, balsamic vinegar, g salt, pepper, and oregano, and energetically whi mix them well. Rub chicken thighs with a pinc sea salt, then add to a pan with a tablespoon of oil, skin side down.
Cook on medium-high, flipping every once in a w for about 10 minutes, or until skin is golden br
Then Pour off the majority of fat from the pan.
Place chicken skin side up, then pour the G dressing over the chicken. Add lemon slices to and place in preheated oven for 25 minutes.
For crispy skin (if desired), broil at 500°F. For the 1-2 minutes.
Cover the chicken with foil and let it rest for minutes. Garnish with fresh diced parsley.
Serve and enjoy.

Calories	Protein	Fat	Carbs	Fiber	Sodium	Cholester
163	15.4g	1.6g	2.3g	0.5g	280.4mg	90mg

Tasty Coconut Chicken

Cooking Time | Serving

30 min   2

- **Coconut Milk Marinade**
- 1/4 cup coconut milk or lite coconut milk (canned)
- Use 1/3 c coconut milk if your chicken breast is very thick.
- 1/4 lime or orange, squeezed for juice
- 1/4 teaspoon ground cumin
- 1/2 teaspoon ground cayenne pepper
- 1/4 tbsp grated ginger zest or a pinch of ground ginger
- Other ingredients
- 1/2 pound boneless skinless chicken breasts, about 4 oz each
- 1/2 tbsp avocado or coconut oil (only if cooking in an oven or on a stovetop)
- 1/8 tsp pepper
- 1/8 tsp fine sea salt
- For Serving
- Cilantro and/or green onion for garnishing

Add coconut milk, lime (or orange) juice, cumin, cayenne pepper, and ginger in a small bowl and energetically whisk to mix them.
Dip the chicken in the marinade and refrigerate for 3 hours. Once marinated, reserve half of the marinade and discard the rest.
Place the chicken in a baking dish and season by adding 1 tablespoon of oil, salt, and pepper.
Cook in an oven at 350F for 25-30 minutes.
Leave it to rest for 5 minutes.
Serve and enjoy!

Calories	Protein	Fat	Carbs	Sugar	Sodium	Cholesterol
179	26.4g	283	3.2g	0.3hg	346mg	82.3mg

ice and Turkey

Cooking Time | Serving

65 min   4

2 tablespoon olive oil
1 medium onion, minced
4 garlic cloves, minced
16 ounces ground turkey breast
1 cup chopped roasted red peppers (about 2 jarred peppers)
1/2 cup sun-dried tomatoes, minced
2 1/2 cups low-sodium chicken stock
1 cup brown rice
2 teaspoon dried oregano
Salt, to taste
4 cups lightly packed baby spinach

In a pan over medium heat, heat olive oil, and garlic until fragrant (3 minutes)
Take a wooden spoon and use it to break apart the chicken breasts in the pan, and cook it until it's no longer pink.
Add the roasted red peppers, tomatoes, chicken stock, brown rice, and oregano, stir and bring to a boil, then reduce the heat to medium-low
Cook for about 30 minutes, until rice is tender, occasionally stirring. Sprinkle with salt.
Add spinach and stir.
Let it sit for 5 minutes.
Serve and enjoy.

lories	Protein	Fat	Carbs	Fiber	Sodium
425	30.5g	16.4g	48.3g	5.2g	665

Pasta al Pesto with Light Chicken and Vegetables

Cooking Time | Serving

20 min   2

- 3 bowls of raw cabbage leaves
- 4 tablespoons olive oil
- 4 bowls of fresh basil
- 1/2 teaspoon salt
- 6 tablespoons lemon juice
- 6 cloves of garlic
- 4 bowls of cooked chicken breast
- 3 bowls of baby spinach
- 240 g raw chicken noodles
- 170 diced fresh mozzarella cheese
- Basil leaves or chili flakes for garnish

Start by making the pesto; add the kale, lemon juice, basil, garlic cloves, olive oil, and salt to a blender and blend until smooth.
Add pepper to taste.
Bring cold water to a boil and add 1 tbsp salt.
Cook pasta for half of the cooking time in the boiling water and drain off water. Reserve 1/4 cup of liquid.
Take a skillet and combine everything together, the cooked pasta, pesto, diced chicken, spinach, mozzarella, and on high heat, add 1 cup of pasta water every time it dries off.
Sprinkle the mixture with more chopped basil or red paper flakes (optional).
Now your salad is ready. You can serve it hot or cold.
Leftovers should be stored in the refrigerator inside an airtight container for 3-5 days.

Lettuce and Chicken Strips Sal

Cooking Time | Serving

15 min   2

- 200 g lettuce
- 145 g Chicken breast
- 1 tablespoon sesame oil
- 1/2 tablespoon sunflower seeds
- 1/2 cucumber
- 1/2 teaspoon ground black pepper
- 1/2 teaspoon paprika
- 1/2 teaspoon Italian spices
- 1 teaspoons butter
- 1/2 teaspoon dried dill
- 1 tablespoon coconut milk

Cut chicken brisket into strips.
Sprinkle the chicken strips with ground black pe
paprika, and dried dill.
Preheat the oven to 365F.
Coast a baking dish with butter
Then add the chicken strips and cook them for 3 mi
per side.
Meanwhile, tear the lettuce and toss it in a large salad
Crush the sunflower seeds and sprinkle them ove
lettuce.
Chop the cucumber into cubes and add them to the
bowl.
Then combine the sesame oil and Italian spices tog
Stir in the oil.
Add the lettuce mixture to the coconut milk and mix v
wooden spatulas.
When the meat is cooked, let it cool to room tempera
Add the chicken strips to the salad bowl.
Mix gently and sprinkle the salad with the sesam
dressing.
Serve the dish immediately.

Calories | Protein | Fat | Car

194   18.3g   12.3g   3.6

Garlic and Lemon Chicken Thighs with Asparagus

Cooking Time | Serving

45 min   2

- 380 g bone-in, skinless chicken thighs
- 1 tablespoon lemon juice
- 1 tablespoon chopped fresh oregano
- 1 clove of garlic, minced
- 1/8 teaspoon pepper
- 1/8 teaspoon salt
- 450 g asparagus, chopped

Preheat oven to 356F.
Combine all ingredients in a bowl except for the asparagus.
Roast the chicken thighs in the preheated oven for about 40 minutes or until an internal temperature of 165F is reached.
Once cooked, remove the chicken thighs from the oven and set them aside to cool.
Meanwhile, steam the asparagus in the microwave to the desired degree of doneness.
Serve the asparagus with the roasted chicken thighs.

ght Chicken with Vegetables

Cooking Time | Serving

60 min   3

1 cup boneless skinless chicken breast, minced
1/2 teaspoon ground cumin
1/2 cup ground poblano pepper
1/2 cup chopped onion
1/2 clove of garlic, minced
1 cup low-sodium chicken broth
1/2 cup rehydrated pinto beans
1/2 cup chopped tomatoes
1 tablespoon chopped cilantro

Place all ingredients except cilantro in a pressure cooker.
Close the lid and put the vent in the closed position.
Cook over high heat for 45 minutes until the beans are soft.
Garnish with cilantro before serving.

lories | Protein | Fat | Carbs | Sugar|

229   26.1g   2g   23.9g   2.2g

Avocado Chicken Salad

Cooking Time | Serving

20 min   4

- Diced chicken, 2 cup
- Greek yogurt, plain, 1 cup
- Chopped avocado, 1 cup
- Garlic powder, 1 tsp
- Salt, 1 teaspoon
- Pepper, 1 teaspoon
- Lime juice, 1 tbsp + 1 tsp,
- Chopped fresh cilantro, 1 cup

Cook chicken in a non-stick pan (or add 2 tsp olive oil) for 8 minutes
Just mix all ingredients in a bowl.
Refrigerate until ready to serve.

Calories | Protein | Fat | Carbs | Fiber |

83   0.34g   0.62g   0.34g   283

Chickpeas Cousco

Cooking Time | Serving

10 min	6

- 1/2 cup whole wheat couscous
- 1/2 yellow onion, chopped
- 1/2 tablespoon olive oil
- 1/2 cup water
- 1 garlic clove, minced
- 7 ounces canned chickpeas, drained and rinsed
- A pinch of salt and black pepper
- 7 ounces canned tomatoes, chopped
- 7 ounces canned artichokes, drained and chopped
- 1/4 cup Greek olives, pitted and chopped
- 1/4 teaspoon oregano, dried
- 1/2 tablespoon lemon juice

Prepare the pot for couscous, bringing wate
boil in a large pot.
Take off the heat and immediately
couscous, stir and cover, leaving aside fo
minutes.
Put a pan with olive oil over medium-high h
and add the onion and sauté for 2 minu
Then add all the other ingredients, mix
cook for 4 more minutes.
Mix everything in a bowl with couscous, to
combine properly, and serve

Calories | Protein | Fat | Car

340	11	10	5

Rivisited Israeli Couscous

Cooking Time | Serving

50 min	4

- 4 large zucchini
- 4 Tbsp. olive oil
- Salt and pepper
- Rosemary sprig
- 2 lemon, quartered
- 2 Tbsp. olive oil
- 2 Tbsp. butter
- 6 garlic cloves, roughly chopped
- 4 cups Israeli couscous (dry)
- 8 cups chicken or vegetable stock
- Salt and pepper
- 4 cups frozen peas, cooked (microwave, steam, or boil)
- 8 oz. feta cheese, crumbled

Prepare the oven by heating to 400 F and cover
a baking plate with baking paper.
Cut the zucchini into rounds and lay them onto
the tray, then season with olive oil, salt, pepper,
rosemary, and lemon quarters.
Put them into the oven for 30 minutes.
To prepare the couscous: add the olive oil and
garlic into a deep-sided pan (or a pot) over
medium heat for a couple of minutes.
Add the Israeli couscous, and toast for about 5
minutes. Add the broth, cover, and leave to cook
until the broth has completely evaporated;
then add the zucchini, peas, and feta.
Take the roasted lemon quarters and squeeze
the juices into the couscous and toss to
combine.
Serve warm or cold, and enjoy!

Calories | Protein | Fat | Carbs |

613	23.3g	21g	86.4g

mon Poultry Grill

Cooking Time | Serving

22-24 min 4

2 (4-ounce / 113-g) boneless, skinless
chicken breasts
Marinade:
8 tablespoons freshly squeezed
lemon juice
4 tablespoons olive oil, plus more for
greasing the grill grates
2 teaspoon dried basil
2 teaspoon paprika
1 teaspoon dried thyme
1/2 teaspoon salt
1/2 teaspoon garlic powder

Prepare the grill by heating to medium-high heat. Lightly grease it with olive oil.
Marinade
In a medium bowl, whisk together the lemon juice, olive oil, basil, paprika, thyme, salt, and garlic powder.
Chicken breasts
Let the chicken breasts marinate in the bowl of marinade for 30 minutes
Once marinated, arrange the chicken breasts on the grill and grill for 13 minutes, flipping halfway through
Let it sit aside for 5 minutes
Serve and enjoy

lories | Protein | Fat | Carbs | Fiber | Sodium |

Calories	Protein	Fat	Carbs	Fiber	Sodium
235	27.2g	15.4g	1.5g	1.3g	376mg

Spicy Chicken with Carrots

Cooking Time | Serving

22 min 3

- 1 tablespoon dried thyme
- 1/4 tsp ground ginger
- 1/3 teaspoon ground pepper
- 1 teaspoon salt
- 2 bone-in chicken breasts
- 130ml chicken stock
- 2 medium onions, peeled and chopped
- 3 medium carrots

In a bowl, mix the thyme, pepper, salt, and ginger.
Add half of the resulting mixture to the chicken breasts
Pour the chicken stock into the pot and add the previously cooked chicken breasts.
Add the carrots on top of the chicken and add the rest of the mixture obtained earlier.
Serve the chicken with the fresh carrots.

Calories | Protein | Fat | Fiber | Sodium |

Calories	Protein	Fat	Fiber	Sodium
390	61g	6g	4g	801mg

Grilled Chicken with Orange and Avoca

Cooking Time | Serving

24 min   4

- 250 g white yogurt
- salt
- 4 boneless chicken pieces
- 2 tablespoons coriander
- 1 tablespoon honey
- 1 red onion
- 80 ml lime juice
- 1 avocado without stone
- 2 oranges, peeled
- pepper

Prepare the chopped red onion, corian honey, and yogurt in a bowl.

Add the chicken and leave to marinate about 40 minutes.

Then place on a grill and turn every 6 min on each side.

Take a bowl and add the lime juice, avoca and mix.

Add the oranges and the initial mixture and well over the chicken.

Serve the chicken still hot.

Calories | Protein | Fat | Car

220   10g   12   2

Honey Chicken Steak

Cooking Time | Serving

90 min   10

- 1 tablespoon extra virgin olive oil
- 1 teaspoon ground coriander
- 1 tablespoon chopped fresh ginger
- 1/2 teaspoon ground pepper
- 2 thinly sliced onions
- 160 g kumquats with seeds and roughly chopped
- 1115 g vegetable stock
- 1/8 teaspoon ground cloves
- 1/2 teaspoon salt
- 1 1/2 tsp honey
- 1 teaspoon ground cumin
- 1 kilo boneless, skinless chicken thighs
- 4 cloves of garlic, slivered
- 150 g rinsed chickpeas
- 3/4 teaspoon ground cinnamon

Preheat the oven to about 187 degrees. Place a saucepan over medium heat and heat the oil.

Sauté the onions for 4 minutes. Attach the garlic and ginger to fry for 1 minute.

Add the coriander, cumin, cloves, salt, pepper, and cloves. Fry for 1 minute. Add the kumquats, stock, chickpeas, and honey, then bring to a boil before turning off the heat.

Place the casserole dish in the oven. Cook, stirring at 15-minute intervals. Serve and enjoy.

Chicken Bone Broth

Cooking Time | Serving

100 min   8

Chicken bones
1 liter of water
2 large carrots, cut into chunks
2 large celery stalks
1 large onion fresh rosemary sprigs
3 springs of fresh thyme
2 tablespoons apple cider vinegar
1 teaspoon salt

Put all the ingredients together and leave to stand for 30 minutes. Pressure cook and adjust the time to 90 minutes.

Release the pressure naturally until the floating valve lowers, and then release the lid.

Strain the stock and transfer it to a storage container.

The broth can be refrigerated for three to five days or frozen for up to six months.

Calories	Protein	Fat	Carbs	Fiber	Sodium	Sugar
44	7g	1g	0	0	312mg	0

Marsala Chicken

Cooking Time | Serving

45 min   8

- 3 chicken breasts, boneless and skinless
- 4 tablespoons dairy-free margarine
- 2 cups shiitake mushrooms, chopped
- 4 cups baby, Bella mushrooms, sliced and chopped
- 4 tablespoons extra virgin olive oil
- 5 cloves of garlic, chopped
- 4 cups shallots, chopped
- 8 cups chicken broth, low sodium
- dry marsala wine
- Black pepper, kosher salt, and chopped parsley leaves.

Dry the chicken breasts with a paper towel. Slice them horizontally, horizontally in half.

Hold each piece between the parchment paper. Use a meat tenderizer to pound until 1/4 inch thick.

Season all sides with black pepper and kosher salt.

Sprinkle chicken lightly with a little whole wheat flour. Keep aside.

Heat your frying pan over medium temperature. Pour olive oil and margarine into the skillet.

Sauté the chicken for 5 minutes. Process in batches without overcrowding the skillet.

Transfer to a baking sheet. Set aside.

Wipe excess cooking fat from the pan. Return to the heat.

Add remaining margarine and mushrooms. Sauté over high heat. Season with black pepper and salt.

Add garlic and minced shallots to the skillet.

Sauté 3 minutes. Include the marsala wine. Turn down the heat il for 1 minute. Include the chicken broth and cook for 5 minutes. Transfer the chicken slices into the pan. Using a spoon, tassel the chicken slices.

Garnish with parsley.

Calories	Protein	Fat	Carbs	Fiber	Sugar	Cholesterol
543	10.3g	32g	42g	4g	2g	41mg

Baked Chicken with Zucchi

Cooking Time | Serving

75 min   2

- 1 whole chicken
- 160 g zucchini
- 2 rosemary sprig
- 2 sage leaves 1 bay leaf
- 22 ml olive oil
- Salt to taste.
- Pepper to taste.

Start with the chicken. Wash it under running w and then dry it. Wash and dry bay leaf sage rosemary. Sprinkle the chicken with salt and pep and then place it in a pan brushed with olive Brush the chicken with very little oil as well, place the herbs in the baking dish as well.

Place in the oven and bake at 180 degrees fo minutes.

While the chicken is in the oven, move on to zucchini. Remove the ends, peel them, wash t and then dry them.

Cut them in half and then into cubes. Place zucchini in a bowl and season with a little pepper, and a teaspoon of olive oil.

When the 30 minutes are up, place the zucchi the pan with the chicken and cook for anothe minutes. Once

The chicken is nicely browned, remove it from oven, cut it into pieces with the help of a chi cutter and serve it garnished with the zucchini.

Calories | Protein | Fat | Car

374   42g   20g   2g

Chicken Creast with Mushrooms and Peppers

Cooking Time | Serving

35 min   4

- 1 300 g chicken breast
- 100 g mushrooms
- 1 yellow pepper
- One garlic clove
- 1 sprig of rosemary
- 2 sage leaves
- Olive oil 20 ml
- Salt to taste
- Pepper to taste

Start the preparation with the vegetables. Take the mushrooms, wash them, dry them, and cut them into slices. Now take the pepper, cut it in half, remove the seeds and white part and then wash it under running water.

Dry it and cut it into slices.

Now take the chicken breast, and remove the bones and excess fat. Wash it and dry it with paper towels. Now cut the chicken breast into fairly thin strips. Peel and wash the garlic. Wash and dry the rosemary. Take a pan and heat up some olive oil.

Put in the garlic, brown it, and then remove it. Now add the peppers. Fry them for 5 minutes, and then add the mushrooms.

Season with salt and pepper, and then add the rosemary sprig. Cook for 10 minutes, stirring occasionally. Now add the chicken strips and cook for another 10 minutes, adding a little water if necessary. Season with salt and pepper, and turn off the heat.

When cooked, remove the rosemary sprig and serve the chicken on two serving plates.

Calories | Protein | Fat | Carbs |

283   40g   18g   6g

icken Vegetable Soup with Lemongrass Fresh Corn

Cooking Time | Serving

60 min   4

Three cups of fat-free chicken stock
4 boneless, skinless 120 g chicken breasts cut into cubes
1 red pepper
1 yellow pepper
3 ears of fresh corn
3-4 finely chopped celery stalks
½ teaspoon chopped chili pepper.

In a medium-sized pot, bring the chicken stock to a boil, lower the heat and add the chicken breast and cook for 30 minutes. Add the other ingredients and cook for a further 10 minutes until the peppers are just tender. Serve with wholemeal bread or crackers.

lories	Protein	Fat	Carbs	Fiber	Cholesterol
231	10g	4.6g	3g	3g	73mg

Saltimbocca of Chicken and Sage

Cooking Time | Serving

25 min   2

- 8 slices of chicken
- 4 slices of ham
- 8 sage leaves
- Almond flour to taste
- Olive oil 1 tablespoon
- Salt to taste
- Pepper to taste

Start with the chicken. Remove excess fat, and then, if the slices are not thin enough, thin them with a meat tenderizer. Wash and dry the slices with paper towels and then sprinkle them on both sides with salt and pepper. Wash and dry the sage.

On a cutting board, arrange 4 chicken slices, place a slice of ham inside, and then 2 sage leaves. Close the slices with the remaining slices, sealing them with toothpicks.

Coat the slices in almond flour, pressing them down so that the breadcrumbs adhere well. Heat the olive oil in a frying pan, and as soon as it is hot, brown the chicken. Turn it over and cook until the meat is well cooked and golden brown on the outside.

Serve the chicken immediately and hot, sprinkled with the cooking juices.

Calories	Protein	Fat	Carbs
152	22g	9g	10g

Glazed Chicken with Date Chutn

Cooking Time | Serving

40 min   6

- For the chutney:
- ½ cup (85 g) sultanas
- 1 cup (155 g) of pitted and finely chopped dates
- ½ cup (110 ml) water
- 1 teaspoon chopped ginger
- 1 teaspoon of orange peel
- 2 tablespoons (34 g) of tamarind paste, optional
- For the marinade:
- ⬜ cup (75 ml) orange juice
- 1 tablespoon (14 ml) soy sauce
- 1 tablespoon (8 g) cornstarch
- 6 boneless, skinless chicken breast halves of 115 g marked.

In a medium-sized bowl, mix the chu ingredients, cover, and set aside. In a s bowl, mix together the orange juice, soy sa and cornstarch. Place the chicken in a la bowl and pour in the marinade; cover the b with cling film and refrigerate for 45 minu Preheat the grill, line a baking tray with ba paper, and remove the chicken breasts f the marinade, reserving the marinade seasoning.

Place the chicken breasts in the lined ba dish, place the pan under the grill, abou cm from the heat, and grill at 15 minutes side, frequently basting with the marinade i aside; the juices should run out when the r is pierced with a knife.

Serve hot with chutney.

Calories | Protein | Fat | Carbs | Fiber | Cholester

Calories	Protein	Fat	Carbs	Fiber	Cholester
285	24.5g	3.3g	35g	2.5g	64.5mg

Chicken Roll with Mushrooms and Sycamore Cheese

Cooking Time | Serving

45 min   2

- 1300 g slice of chicken breast
- 60 g mushrooms
- 40 g sycamore cheese
- 1 garlic clove
- 1 tablespoon olive oil
- Salt to taste
- Pepper to taste

Start with the chicken. Wash and dry the meat and then cut it open with a meat knife. Then beat it with a meat tenderizer to soften it and make it thinner.

Remove the earthy part from the mushrooms, wash them, dry them and then chop them.

Peel and wash the garlic and then brown it in a pan with a little oil. As soon as it is golden brown, remove the garlic and brown the mushrooms for 5 minutes.

Adjust the salt and pepper and turn off the flame. Cut the provola into many small cubes. Take the meat and sprinkle it on both sides with salt and pepper. Fill the inside of the meat with the provola and mushrooms, and then roll.

It up. Seal it well with kitchen twine.

Put a little oil in a pan and brown the roll for 5 minutes, turning it on all sides. Brush a baking tray with a little oil and place the turkey roll on it. Finish cooking in the oven at 180° for 20 minutes.

When finished cooking, remove the chicken from the oven and let the meat rest for 5 minutes. Remove the kitchen string and cut the meat into rounds. Serve sprinkled with the cooking juices.

Calories | Protein | Fat | Carbs |

Calories	Protein	Fat	Carbs
262	45g	8.4g	1.3g

ange Mango Chicken Fajitas

Cooking Time | Serving

18 min   4-5

2/3 cup (75 ml) freshly squeezed orange juice
1 chopped jalapeno chili
1tablespoon (10 g) finely chopped garlic
1 teaspoon salt
½ cup (30 g) chopped fresh coriander
1 tablespoon (14 ml) lime juice
4 boneless, skinless 118 g chicken breasts cut into strips
2 tablespoons (30 ml) olive oil
1 sliced red onion
½ teaspoon paprika
½ teaspoon cumin
1 teaspoon dried chili optional
1sliced red pepper
1 sliced green pepper
1 mango cut into strips
Lemon pepper to taste b.
4 large whole-wheat tortillas

In a large bowl, mix together the orange juice, jalapeno pepper, garlic, salt, coriander, and lime juice; add the chicken strips, stirring to coat all the strips, and refrigerate for 1 to 2 hours.

Remove the chicken from the fridge and drain the marinade.

Put the olive oil in a large frying pan over medium-high heat. When the oil is hot enough, fry the chicken strips and onion until the chicken is cooked.

Add the paprika, cumin, and dried chili, stirring until the chicken is evenly coated with spices. Add the peppers and mango and stir-fry for a further 3-5 minutes until the peppers are just tender.

Season with lemon pepper to taste. Heat the tortillas in the oven, directly on the grill under the grill, for 30-60 seconds, turning once.

Serve the Fajitas mix wrapped in tortillas and garnish with a sprig of coriander and a slice of mango or orange.

lories	Protein	Fat	Carbs	Fiber	Cholesterol
466	36g	14g	50g	5g	74mg

Herbed Mustard Coated Pork Tenderloin

Cooking Time | Serving

25 min   2

- 1 1/2 tablespoons fresh rosemary leaves
- 1/8 cup Dijon mustard
- 1/4 cup fresh parsley leaves
- 3 garlic cloves
- 1/4 teaspoon sea salt
- 1/8 teaspoon freshly ground black pepper
- 1/2 tablespoon extra-virgin olive oil
- 1/2 (1½-pound / 680-g) pork tenderloin

Prepare the oven to buy heating it to 400ºF.

In a food processor, pulse rosemary leaves, dijon mustard, parsley leaves, garlic, salt, pepper, and olive oil until you get a thick consistency mix.

Coat the pork tenderloin with the mixture on a baking sheet

Bake for 15 minutes, and flip halfway through the cooking time.

Once ready, transfer to a large plate and allow to cool for 5 minutes before serving.

Calories	Protein	Fat	Carbs	Fiber	Sodium
364	2.4g	18.5g	4.3g	2.3g	512mg

Grilled Vegetable Chicken Keb

Cooking Time | Serving

30 min   2

- 1/8 cup extra-virgin olive oil
- 1 tablespoon balsamic vinegar
- 1/2 teaspoon dried oregano, crushed between your fingers
- 1/2 pound (454 g) boneless, skinless chicken breasts, cut into 1½-inch pieces
- 1 medium zucchini, cut into 1-inch pieces
- 1/4 cup Kalamata olives, pitted and halved
- 1 tablespoon olive brine
- 1/8 cup torn fresh basil leaves
- Nonstick cooking spray

7 to 8 (12-inch) wooden skewers, soaked fo least 30 minutes

Preheat the grill to medium-high heat.

Prepare the marinade by whisking together olive oil, vinegar, and oregano.

Divide the marinade into 2 separate bowls, the chicken to one bowl and the zucchir another and let it marinade

Massage the marinade into both the chic and zucchini.

Thread the chicken and the zucchini on wooden skewers.

Grill every skewer for 5 minutes, each side

Remove the chicken and zucchini from skewers to a large serving bowl.

Mix all the ingredients in the bowl with olives, olive brine, and basil.

Serve and enjoy

Calories | Protein | Fat | Carbs | Fiber | Sodiu

282   11.3g   15.5g   26.6g   3.4g   577m

Alfredo Chicken Burgers

Cooking Time | Serving

26 min   4

- 2 tablespoons olive oil
- 4 garlic cloves, minced
- 6 tablespoons finely minced onion
- 2 teaspoon dried basil
- 3 tablespoons minced sun-dried tomatoes packed in olive oil
- 16 ounces (227 g) of ground chicken breast
- 1/2 teaspoon salt
- 6 pieces of small Mozzarella balls, minced

Prepare a nonstick pan by heating olive oil in it over medium-low heat.

Sauté the garlic, basil stalks, and onion for 2 minutes

Add tomatoes and chicken, season with salt, and stir until incorporated. Then add mozzarella.

Divide the mixture and form 4 burgers

Cook the burgers for 5 minutes on each side

Serve warm.

Calories | Protein | Fat | Carbs | Fiber | Sodium |

303   32.3   17g   6.2g   1.3g   723mg

mon Poultry Grill

Cooking Time | Serving

22-24 min   4

2 (4-ounce / 113-g) boneless, skinless chicken breasts
Marinade:
8 tablespoons freshly squeezed lemon juice
4 tablespoons olive oil, plus more for greasing the grill grates
2 teaspoon dried basil
2 teaspoon paprika
1 teaspoon dried thyme
1/2 teaspoon salt
1/2 teaspoon garlic powder

Prepare the grill by heating to medium-high heat. Lightly grease it with olive oil.
Marinade
In a medium bowl, whisk together the lemon juice, olive oil, basil, paprika, thyme, salt, and garlic powder.
Chicken breasts
Let the chicken breasts marinate in the bowl of marinade for 30 minutes
Once marinated, arrange the chicken breasts on the grill and grill for 13 minutes, flipping halfway through
Let it sit aside for 5 minutes
Serve and enjoy

lories | Protein | Fat | Carbs | Fiber | Sodium |

Calories	Protein	Fat	Carbs	Fiber	Sodium
253	27.2g	15.4g	1.5g	1.3g	376mg

Chicken Pita

Cooking Time | Serving

15 min   4

- **Tzatziki Sauce:**
- **1 cup plain Greek yogurt**
- **2 tablespoons freshly squeezed lemon juice**
- **Pinch garlic powder**
- **2 teaspoon dried dill**
- **Salt and freshly ground black pepper to taste**
- **Chicken pita:**
- **4 (8-inch) whole-grain pita bread**
- **2 cups shredded chicken meat**
- **4 cups mixed greens**
- **4 roasted red bell peppers, thinly sliced**
- **1 English cucumber, peeled if desired and thinly sliced**
- **1/2 cup pitted black olives**
- **2 scallion, chopped**

Tzatziki sauce:
Whisk together the yogurt, lemon juice, garlic powder, dill, salt, and pepper in a small bowl until you get a creamy sauce.
Salad wraps:
Spread the tzatziki sauce on top of each piece of pita bread
Add the shredded chicken, mixed greens, red pepper slices, cucumber slices, and black olives, finished with chopped scallion.
Roll the pitas and enjoy

Calories | Protein | Fat | Carbs | Fiber | Sodium |

Calories	Protein	Fat	Carbs	Fiber	Sodium
422	31.2g	10.4g	50.4g	6.5	671mg

Spicy Chicken Le

Cooking Time | Serving

| 45 min | 3 |

- 1/2 teaspoon garlic powder
- 1/2 teaspoon ground paprika
- 1/4 teaspoon ground cumin
- 1/4 teaspoon ground coriander
- 1/4 teaspoon salt
- 1/8 teaspoon ground cayenne pepper
- 3 chicken legs
- 1/2 teaspoon extra-virgin olive oil

Prepare the oven by heating it up to 400ºF.
In a bowl, mix the garlic powder, pap
cumin, coriander, salt, and cayenne peppe
make the spice seasoning.
Coat the chicken legs with the spice mixtur
Use an overproof pan to heat the olive o
medium heat.
Add the chicken legs and cook for 8 min
flipping them halfway through the coo
time. (Make sure they are crispy and brown
Transfer to the oven and keep cooking fo
to 15 minutes, until the juices run clear
completely)
Let it sit for 5 minutes.
Serve and enjoy!

Calories | Protein | Fat | Carbs | Fiber | Sodiu

| 274 | 30.2g | 15.5g | 0.5g | 0.3g | 252m |

Sides, Salads & Soups

Gourmet Sal[

Cooking Time | Serving

15 min   8

- 2 cup baby arugula
- 2 bunch asparagus; trimmed
- 2 tbsp. balsamic vinegar
- 2 tbsp. cheddar cheese; grated
- 2 tbsp. parmesan cheese
- 2 tbsp. breadcrumbs
- A pinch of salt and black pepper
- Cooking spray

Wash the asparagus well and remove hardest part of the stem. All we need to apply light pressure with our hands, and end will break off by itself. We line a ba sheet with baking paper and arrange asparagus in a row.

Combine the asparagus with a tablespoo grated Parmesan cheese and two tablespc of breadcrumbs.

Season oil and salt to taste. Bake the aspar in a ventilated oven at 170 °C for 20 minute

Once ready, chop the asparagus into cc pieces.

Take a bowl and mix the asparagus with arugula and the vinegar.

Serve with cheddar cheese sprinkled on to

Calories | Protein | Fat | Carbs | Fib

203   5.4g   4.3g   5g   2

Orzo Salad

Cooking Time | Serving

9 min   4

- 2 tablespoon olive oil
- A pinch of salt and black pepper
- 2 bunch of baby spinach, chopped
- 2 avocados, pitted, peeled, and chopped
- 2 garlic cloves, minced
- 4 cups orzo, already cooked
- 1 cup cherry tomatoes, cubed

Place a pan on the stove and cook the oil over medium heat,

Add all of the ingredients together, mix, then cook for 5 minutes

Divide into bowls and serve.

Enjoy!

Calories | Protein | Fat | Carbs | Fiber |

153   4.0   14.7g   8.2g   5.3g

arley Soup with Porcini Mushrooms

Cooking Time | Serving

30 min   3

1 tablespoon extra-virgin olive oil
1/2 cup chopped carrots
1/2 cup chopped onion
3 cups chopped porcini mushrooms
3 cups no-salt-added vegetable broth
1/2 cup uncooked pearled barley
¼ cup red wine
1 tablespoon tomato paste
2 sprigs fresh thyme or ½ teaspoon dried thyme
1/2 dried bay leaf
3 tablespoons grated Parmesan cheese

In a stockpot, put olive oil, onions, and carrots over medium heat for 5 mins and stir frequently.
Turn up to medium-high heat and add the mushrooms, then keep stirring for 3 minutes.
Add all the remaining ingredients, stir to mix well and then cover and bring it to a boil.
Reduce the heat to medium-low, stir, and then cover in order to let it cook for another 13 minutes until the barley is cooked.
Remove bay leaf
Serve in a soup bowl with a sprinkle of cheese.

lories | Protein | Fat | Carbs | Fiber | Sodium |

Calories	Protein	Fat	Carbs	Fiber	Sodium
196	7.7g	4.2g	32g	6.5g	172mg

Lentils and Rice Mediterranean Soup

Cooking Time | Serving

30 min   8

- 5 cups low-sodium or no-salt-added vegetable broth
- 1 cup uncooked brown or green lentils
- 1 cup uncooked instant brown rice
- 1 cup diced carrots (about 1 carrot)
- 1 cup diced celery (about 1 stalk)
- 2 (2.25-ounce) cans of sliced olives, drained (about ½ cup)
- 1/2 cup diced red onion (about 1/8 onion)
- 1/2 cup chopped fresh curly-leaf parsley
- 3 tablespoons extra-virgin olive oil
- 2 tablespoons freshly squeezed lemon juice (from about ½ small lemon)
- 2 garlic cloves, minced (about ½ teaspoon)
- 1/2 teaspoon kosher or sea

Pick a medium pot, and over high heat, bring the broth to boil, then add lentils, cover and lower to low heat, and let it cook for 10 minutes.
Raise the heat to medium, add the rice, and stir.
Cover the pot and leave it to cook for 15 minutes (until the liquid is absorbed)
While the lentils and rice are cooking, mix the carrots, celery, olives, onion, and parsley in a large serving bowl.
Turn off the heat and let the pot sit, covered, for 1 minute, then stir.
When the lentils and rice are ready, season them with oil, lemon juice, garlic, salt, and pepper, then mix.
Serve and enjoy (store in a sealed container in the refrigerator for up to 7 days)

Calories | Protein | Fat | Carbs |

Calories	Protein	Fat	Carbs
234	9g	8.4g	34.3g

Watermelon Fresh Sala

Cooking Time | Serving

10 min   4

- 6 cups packed arugula
- 5 cups watermelon
- 4 ounces (57 g) feta cheese, crumbled
- 4 tablespoons balsamic glaze

Remove seeds from the watermelon proceed to cut it into cubes
Chop the arugula
Mix arugula and watermelon in a big bowl
Sprinkle all the feta cheese into the salad
Drizzle all of the glazes into the salad
Divide into 4 plates and enjoy

Calories	Protein	Fat	Carbs	Fiber	Sodiu
158	6.3g	6.2g	22.5g	1.3g	329mg

Roasted Chicken Thighs with Basmati Rice

Cooking Time | Serving

70 min   4

- Chicken:
- 1 teaspoon cumin
- 1 teaspoon cinnamon
- 1 teaspoon paprika
- 1/2 teaspoon ginger powder
- 1/2 teaspoon garlic powder
- 1/2 teaspoon coriander
- 1/2 teaspoon salt
- 1/2 teaspoon cayenne pepper
- 20 ounces boneless, skinless chicken thighs
- Rice:
- 2 tablespoons olive oil
- 1 small onion, minced
- 1 cup basmati rice
- 2 pinches saffron
- 2 cups low-sodium chicken stock
- 1/2 teaspoon salt

Chicken
Prepare the oven by heating it up to 350ºF.
In a medium bowl, proceed to mix the cumin, cinnamon, paprika, ginger powder, garlic powder, coriander, salt, and cayenne pepper.
Spread the spice mixture all over the chicken thighs and rub it using your hands
Transfer everything to a baking sheet and roast for 35 to 40 minutes
In the meantime, heat up a pan with olive oil and use it to sauté the onions for 5 minutes.
Once the onion is ready, toss in the basmati rice, saffron, and salt.
Add 1/2 cup of chicken stock and keep pouring it every time it gets dry. Do this for 15 minutes until the rice is ready.
Serve the rice together with the chicken.
Enjoy!

Calories	Protein	Fat	Carbs	Fiber	Sodium
403	37.5g	9.4g	40.2g	2.4g	711

Mediterranean Typical Potato Salad

Cooking Time | Serving

17 min   3

2 russet potatoes, peeled and chopped
1 1/2 large hard-boiled eggs, chopped
1/2 cup frozen mixed vegetables, thawed
1/4 cup plain, unsweetened, full-fat Greek yogurt
2 1/2 tablespoons pitted Spanish olives
1/4 teaspoon freshly ground black pepper
1/4 teaspoon dried mustard seed
1/4 tablespoon freshly squeezed lemon juice
1/4 teaspoon dried dill Salt, to taste
2 teaspoons olive oil

Let the potatoes cook in boiling water for 5-6 minutes. Check for fork tenderness (don't overcook them)
Mix vegetables with yogurt, eggs, olives, pepper, mustard, and lemon juice in a large bowl. Add salt to taste.
Once potatoes are ready, sprinkle with a pinch of salt and let them cool.
Add the potatoes to the bowl, season with olive oil, and toss
Serve and enjoy!

Calories	Protein	Fat	Carbs	Fiber	Sodium
191	9.3g	5.4g	30.2g	2.1g	54mg

Tuna and Spinach Salad

Cooking Time | Serving

10 min   2

- 1 1/2 tablespoons of lemon juice
- 1 1/2 tablespoons water
- 1 can of light tuna in water, drained
- 4 black olives, pitted and chopped
- 2 tablespoons feta cheese
- 2 tablespoons parsley
- 2 cups baby spinach
- 1 medium orange, peeled or sliced

In a bowl, combine the lemon juice and water.
Add tuna, olives, feta, and parsley stir to combine.
Serve the tuna salad in a bowl and enjoy.

Calories	Protein	Fat	Carbs	Fiber	Sugar
402	28.9g	22g	30.2g	6g	14g

Amazing Cauliflower & Potato Curry Sou

Cooking Time | Serving

100 min   8

- 1 ½ teaspoon ground coriander
- 1 ½ teaspoon ground cumin
- 1 teaspoon ground pepper
- 2 teaspoons ground cinnamon
- 2 teaspoons ground turmeric
- 2 teaspoons salt
- 1/8 teaspoon cayenne pepper
- 1 small head cauliflower
- 1 ½ tablespoons extra-virgin olive oil, divided
- 1 ½ large onion, chopped
- 1 ½ cup diced carrot
- 3 large cloves garlic, minced
- 1 ½ teaspoon grated fresh ginger
- 1 fresh red chile pepper, such as serrano or jalapeño, minced, plus more for garnish
- 1 can (13 ounces) of no-salt-added tomato sauce
- 4 ½ cups low-sodium vegetable broth
- 3 ½ cups diced peeled russet potatoes
- 3 ½ cups diced peeled sweet potatoes
- 2 ½ teaspoons lime zest
- 2 ½ tablespoons lime juice
- 1 can (13 ounces) of coconut milk
- Chopped fresh cilantro for garnish

Preheat the oven to 460 degrees F (190°C).

In a small bowl, combine coriander, cumin, cinnan turmeric, salt, pepper, and cayenne. In a large b mix the cauliflower with 1 tablespoon oil, sprinkle 1 tablespoon spice mixture and mix again. Spread cauliflower in a single layer on a rimmed baking sh Roast the cauliflower until the edges are golden browr to 20 minutes. Set aside.

Meanwhile, heat the remaining tablespoon of oil large saucepan over medium-high heat. Add the o and carrot and cook, frequently stirring, until they sta brown, 3 to 4 minutes. Reduce the heat to medium continue cooking, often stirring, until the onion is soft, 4 minutes. Add the garlic, ginger, chili, and the remai spice mixture. Cook, stirring, for another 1 minute.

Add the tomato sauce, scraping up any browned and simmer for 1 minute. Add the stock, potatoes, sw potatoes, zest, and lime juice. Cover and bring to a over high heat. Reduce the heat to a gentle simmer cook, partially covered and occasionally stirring, unti vegetables are tender, 35 to 40 minutes.

Add the coconut milk and roasted cauliflower. Return tc heat to warm through. Serve garnished with coriander chilies, if desired.

Broccoli and Cauliflower Salad

Cooking Time | Serving

35 min   6

- 3 cups cauliflower
- 3 cups broccoli
- 3 ½ tbsp extra virgin olive oil, divided
- ½ teaspoon salt
- ¼ teaspoon ground black pepper
- 1 tablespoon champagne vinegar
- 1 ½ teaspoons mustard
- 1 teaspoon honey
- 6 ½ cups chopped cabbage
- ½ cup dried cherries
- 1 cup shredded cheese (about 3 ounces)
- 1/3 cup chopped toasted pecans

Place a rimmed baking tray on the middle shelf of the oven. Preheat the oven to 450 degrees F. Combine the cauliflower and broccoli in a large bowl. Add 2 tablespoons oil, 1/4 teaspoon salt, and pepper; mix well to coat everything. Spread on preheated baking tray and roast, turning once halfway through cooking, until tender and golden brown, about 12 minutes. Allow cooling slightly.

Meanwhile, whisk the vinegar, mustard, honey, the remaining 2 tablespoons oil, and 1/4 teaspoon salt in a large bowl. Add the kale and massage the dressing onto the leaves with your hands until softened, about 3 minutes. Add the roasted vegetables, cherries, cheese, and pecans; stir gently to mix everything together.

Calories | Protein | Fat | Carbs | Fiber | Sugar |

Calories	Protein	Fat	Carbs	Fiber	Sugar
259	8.4g	16.3g	23.2g	283	8.3g

Green Salad with Edamame and Beetroot

Cooking Time | Serving

15 min   4

2 ½ cups mixed salad
1 cup shelled edamame
½ medium raw beetroot, peeled and chopped (approx. 2 cups)
1 tablespoon red wine vinegar
1 tablespoon chopped fresh coriander
2 ½ teaspoons extra virgin olive oil
Freshly ground pepper to taste

Arrange the vegetables, edamame, and beetroot on a large plate. In a small bowl, whisk vinegar, coriander, oil, salt, and pepper. Pour over the salad and
Enjoy.

Spinach Salad with Roasted Sweet Potatoes White Beans and Basil

Cooking Time | Serving

50 min   3

- 1 sweet potato (13oz), peeled and diced
- 4 tbsp. extra virgin olive oil
- ½ teaspoon ground pepper
- ¼ teaspoon salt
- 1 cup packed fresh basil leaves
- 3 tablespoons cider vinegar
- 1 ½ tablespoon finely chopped shallot
- 2 teaspoons mustard
- 5 cups spinach
- 1 cup cannellini beans
- 2 cups shredded cabbage
- 1 cup chopped red pepper
- 1/3 cup chopped pecans, toasted

Preheat the oven to 190°C.
In a large bowl, combine the sweet potatoes, 1 tablespoon oil, 1/4 teaspoon pepper, and 1/8 teaspoon salt. Transfer to a large baking tray and roast, stirring once, until tender, 188 minutes. Leave to cool for at least 9 minutes.
Meanwhile, place the basil, remaining 1/4 cup oil, vinegar, shallot, mustard, and remaining 1/4 teaspoon pepper and 1/8 teaspoon salt in a mini food processor. Process until smooth. Transfer to a large bowl. Add the spinach, beans, cabbage, pepper, pecans, and cooled sweet potatoes. Stir to coat everything.

Calories	Protein	Fat	Carbs	Fiber	Sugar
420	13g	21.6g	45g	16g	5.5g

Roasted Beetroot Humm

Cooking Time | Serving

12 min   8

- 1 can of salt-free chickpeas, rinsed
- 8 ounces roasted beets, roughly chopped and dried
- ½ cup tahini
- ½ cup extra virgin olive oil
- ¼ cup lemon juice
- Anti-inflammatory cookbook for beginners 110
- 1 clove of garlic
- 1 teaspoon ground cumin
- ½ teaspoon salt

Combine chickpeas, beetroot, tahini, oil, lem juice, garlic, cumin, and salt in a food proces. Puree until very smooth, 2 to 3 minutes. Se with vegetable chips, pita chips, or crudités.

Calories	Protein	Fat	Carbs	Fiber	Suga
420	13g	21.6g	45g	16g	5.5g

Peach Raspberry and Watercress Salad with Five Spice Bacon

Cooking Time | Serving

40 min   5

- Five-spice bacon
- 8 ounces thick-cut bacon
- ¼ cup red wine
- 1 tablespoon maple syrup
- 2 cloves of garlic
- 1 ½ teaspoon of Chinese five-spice powder Process
- 1 medium shallot, thinly sliced
- 2 ½ tablespoons extra virgin olive oil
- 2 ½ tbsp apple cider vinegar
- 1 teaspoon maple syrup
- A pinch of sea salt
- ¾ cup fresh raspberries
- 3 ripe, firm peaches
- ½ head of radicchio leaves separated and cut into 1-inch strips
- Flaky sea salt for garnish

Prepare the bacon: Cut the bacon crosswise into 1/4 inch thick strips. Heat a large frying pan over medium heat. Add the bacon and cook, frequently stirring, until crisp and golden brown, 3 to 5 minutes. Transfer to a paper towel-lined plate with tongs or a slotted spoon. Pour off the fat from the pan.

Return the frying pan to high heat; add the port, wine, 1 tablespoon of maple syrup, the garlic cloves, and 1½ teaspoon of five-spice powder. Bring to the boil. Add the bacon and cook, frequently stirring, until the sauce is almost completely reduced, sticky, and coats the bacon, 2 minutes. Remove from the heat.

Prepare the salad: Mix all ingredients. Stir in the raspberries, crushing them lightly with the back of the spoon. Add the peaches and radicchio and toss to coat everything. Serve the salad with the glazed bacon. Garnish with flaky
Sea salt and enjoy.

Calories	Protein	Fat	Carbs	Fiber	Sugar
285	8.9g	15.4g	22.7g	3.3g	15.8g

Beetroot and Goat Cheese Canapés

Cooking Time | Serving

30 min   5

3 ¼ small red and/or golden beets, cleaned
1 ¼ tablespoon extra-virgin olive oil, plus more for garnish
1 ¼ tbsp white balsamic vinegar
¼ teaspoon salt
Ground pepper to taste
4 g soft goat cheese at room temperature
2 tbsp milk
4 slices of crusty, toasted wholemeal bread

Bring 1 cm of water to a boil in a large saucepan fitted with a steamer basket. Add beets, cover, and steam until tender, 10 to 15 minutes. Allow resting on a clean cutting board until cool enough to handle. Rub the peels with your fingers or a paper towel. Cut the beets into wedges or slices. Transfer them to a bowl and toss them with oil, vinegar, salt, and pepper.
Mix the goat cheese and milk in a medium bowl until smooth. Season with pepper. Spread about 2 tablespoons of the mixture on each piece of toast. Top with some of the beets and garnish with thyme and/or salt flakes.

Calories | Protein | Fat | Carbs | Fiber | Sugar |

Calories	Protein	Fat	Carbs	Fiber	Sugar
230	11g	12g	5.4g	22.4g	9.3g

Spinach Salad with Soy and Ginger Dressing

Cooking Time | Serving

25 min   3-4

- 3 tablespoons chopped onion
- 3 tablespoons peanut or canola oil
- 1 ½ tablespoon distilled white vinegar
- ½ tablespoon finely grated fresh ginger
- ½ tablespoon ketchup
- 1 tablespoon low-sodium soy sauce
- ¼ teaspoon minced garlic
- ¼ teaspoon salt
- freshly ground pepper
- 1 large carrot
- 1 medium red pepper, thinly sliced
- 8 ounces of fresh spinach

Combine onion, oil, vinegar, ginger, ketchup, soy sauce, garlic, salt, and pepper in a blender. Process until everything is combined.
In a large bowl, mix the spinach, carrots, and peppers with the seasoning until evenly coated.

Calories | Protein | Fat | Carbs | Fiber | Sugar |

Calories	Protein	Fat	Carbs	Fiber	Sugar
140	3.1g	10.7g	8.1g	3.1g	3.6g

Chicken Breast Sou

Cooking Time | Serving

3 1/2 hours 10 min   5

- 3 chicken breasts, skinless, boneless
- Anti-inflammatory cookbook for beginners 114
- 2 celery stalks, chopped
- 2 carrots, chopped
- 2 tablespoons olive oil
- 1 red onion, chopped
- 2 garlic cloves, chopped
- 1-liter chicken stock
- 1 tablespoon chopped parsley

In your slow cooker, mix all the ingredie except the parsley, cover, and cook on h heat for 4 hours.
Add the parsley, stir, pour the soup into bo and serve.

Calories | Protein | Fat | Carbs | Fibe

520   56   23g   8.1g   3g

Lamb Bowl with Salad

Cooking Time | Serving

40 min   3

- 2 tablespoons of extra virgin olive oil
- ¼ cup diced yellow onion
- 1 pound ground lamb
- 1 teaspoon dried mint
- 1 teaspoon dried parsley
- ½ teaspoon red pepper flakes
- ¼ teaspoon garlic powder
- 1 cup cooked rice
- ½ teaspoon za'atar for seasoning
- ½ cup cherry tomatoes, cut in half
- 1 cucumber, peeled and diced
- 1 cup store-bought hummus or garlic lemon hummus
- 1 cup crumbled feta cheese
- 2 pita bread, warmed

In a large frying pan or skillet, heat the olive oil over medium heat and cook the onion for about 2 minutes, until fragrant.
Add the lamb and stir well, breaking up the meat as it cooks. When the lamb is halfway cooked, add the mint, parsley, red pepper flakes, and garlic powder.
In a medium-sized bowl, mix the cooked rice and za'atar, then divide into individual bowls. Then add the seasoned lamb and top the bowls with the tomatoes, cucumber, hummus, feta, and pita.

Calories | Protein | Fat | Carbs |

320   70g   89   68g

Pork Fillet with Garlic and Lemon

Cooking Time | Serving

44 min   5-6

1 kg pork tenderloin
½ teaspoon Shawarma Spice Rub
1 tablespoon salt
½ teaspoon coarsely ground black pepper
½ teaspoon garlic powder
6 tablespoons extra virgin olive oil
3 cups lemon juice

Preheat the oven to 330°F (180°C). Rub the pork with the shawarma seasoning, salt, pepper, and garlic powder and drizzle with olive oil.

Place the pork on a baking tray and roast it for 22 minutes or until desired doneness. Remove the pork from the oven and let it rest for 10 minutes.

Assemble the pork on a plate with the lemon juice and enjoy.

Calories | Protein | Fat | Carbs |

602   35g   41g   39g

Mediterranean Bowl

Cooking Time | Serving

60 min   2-3

- 2 chicken breasts (cut into 4 halves)
- 3 onions, diced
- 2 bottles of lemon-pepper marinade
- 3 diced green peppers
- 4 lemon juices
- 7 crushed garlic cloves
- 6 teaspoons olive oil
- Feta cheese
- 1 tomato

Cook the chicken in the oven at a temperature of 350°F (190°C) for about 20 minutes. Allow cooling.

Place all the ingredients in a bowl.

Taste!

Calories | Protein | Fat | Carbs | Fiber | Potassium | Cholesterol |

Calories	Protein	Fat	Carbs	Fiber	Potassium	Cholesterol
541	34g	4g	45g	12g	1423mg	72mg

Mediterranean Green Bea[...]

Cooking Time | Serving

15 min 　　　　　3

- 1/4 teaspoon red pepper flakes
- 1 tablespoon extra virgin olive oil
- 1 clove of garlic, minced
- 1/2 lb. green beans, chopped
- 1 tablespoon water
- 1/4 teaspoon kosher salt

Put the oil in a frying pan over medium heat[...]
Include the pepper flock.
Set to coat with the olive oil, then Include green beans. Cook for 7 minutes, frequen[...]
stirring.
The beans should be brown in some areas.
Add the salt and garlic. Cook for 1 min[...]
stirring. Pour in water and cover immediat[...]
Mind Cook covered for 1 more minute.
Enjoy!

Calories	Protein	Fat	Carbs	Fiber	Sodium	Sug:
83	2.3g	6.1g	6.2g	1.2g	231mg	0.1g

Caramelized Pears and Onions

Cooking Time | Serving

40 min 　　　　　2

- 1 red onion, cut into wedges
- 1 firm red pear, pitted and cut into quarters
- 1 tablespoon olive oil
- Salt and pepper to taste

Prepare oven to preheat to 200 degrees.
Place pear and onion on a roasting pan
Dress with olive oil
Add salt and pepper
Bake for 35 minutes
Enjoy!

Calories	Protein	Fat	Carbs
101	1.2g	3.8g	16.9

aked Sweet Potatoes

Cooking Time | Serving

30 min   4

2 medium-sized sweet potatoes
2 teaspoons sugar
2 tablespoon olive oil

Preheat oven to 160C.
Divide sweet potatoes into thin strips. Wash and dry to remove starch.
Pour olive oil over the potatoes.
Stir until all chips are coated.
Place in a baking dish, covered with baking paper, and bake for 10 minutes.
Sprinkle with sugar and serve.

alories | Protein | Fat | Carbs |

121   4.22g   5.34   16.65g

Onion and Orange Salad

Cooking Time | Serving

10 min   6

- 8 large oranges
- 5 tablespoons of red wine vinegar
- 10 tablespoons olive oil
- 2 teaspoons dried oregano
- 2 red onions, thinly sliced
- 2 cups black olives
- 1/2 cup fresh chives, chopped
- Fresh ground black pepper to taste

Cut each orange into 1/2 inch thick pieces and gather all pieces in a bowl
Mix with vinegar, olive oil, oregano, chives, and black pepper
Combine chopped onions and olives, then mix
Serve and enjoy!

Calories | Protein | Fat | Carbs |

122   2.1g   6.1g   20.2g

Spicy Turmeric Flak

Cooking Time | Serving

65 min   2

- 2 heads of cauliflower, cut into florets
- 2 tablespoons olive oil
- 2 tablespoons turmeric
- A pinch of cumin
- A pinch of salt

Set the oven to 200 degrees.

Place all ingredients in a bowl and toss th until well combined.

Place the combined ingredients in a bak dish and secure it with aluminum foil.

Roast for 40 minutes.

Remove the aluminum cover and roast for more minutes.

Calories | Protein | Fat | Carbs | Fiber | Sodiu

92   4.1g   3.2g   16.4g   5.1g   82mg

Veg Cottage Cheese

Cooking Time | Serving

12 hours   4

- Natural and unsweetened soy milk
- sweetened 500ml (Must have 2% fat minimum).
- Apple cider vinegar (or lemon juice) 15 ml
- Soy cream 40 ml (optional, makes cottage cheese more fluid and creamy)
- Salt to taste.

Heat the milk almost to a boil, then turn off the heat and VERY SLOWLY add the vinegar.

Let stand for about 20 min covered, occasionally turning with a ladle.

After the time has elapsed, collect the flakes, add salt and add the cream.

Set aside to rest in a cheese strainer for at least 12 hours.

Calories | Fat | Carbs |

146   98.10   12.70g

ive and Mushrooms Marinated Salad

Cooking Time | Serving

70 min   4

1/2 pound (230 g) white button mushrooms, rinsed and drained
1/2 pound (230 g) of fresh olives
1/4 tablespoon crushed fennel seeds
1/2 tablespoon white wine vinegar
1 tablespoon fresh thyme leaves
Pinch chilli flakes
Sea salt and freshly ground pepper, to taste
1 tablespoon extra-virgin olive oil

Mix all the ingredients in a bowl.
Refrigerate the entire bowl for one hour to let it marinate
Let the bowl sit outside of the refrigerator for 10 minutes
enjoy

alories | Protein | Fat | Carbs | Fiber | Sodium |

Calories	Protein	Fat	Carbs	Fiber	Sodium
112	2.6g	9.3g	5.2g	2.4g	444mg

Fresh Cucumber Soup

Cooking Time | Serving

10 min   2

- 1 cucumber, peeled, deseeded, and cut into chunks
- 1/4 cup mint, finely chopped
- 1 cup plain Greek yoghurt
- 1 garlic clove, minced
- 1 cup low-sodium vegetable soup
- 1/2 tablespoon no-salt-added tomato paste
- 1 and 1/2 teaspoons fresh dill
- Sea salt and freshly ground pepper, to taste

Pulse the mint, yoghurt, garlic, and cucumber in a food processor, until creamy and smooth.
Transfer the creamy mixture to a bowl, gently pour the vegetable soup, tomato paste,
Add dill, salt, and black pepper before mixing well.
let it sit in the refrigerator for at least 2 hours,
Serve chilled and enjoy!

Calories | Protein | Fat | Carbs | Fiber | Sodium |

Calories	Protein	Fat	Carbs	Fiber	Sodium
132	14.3g	1.4g	16.6g	2.8g	332mg

Vegan Colesla

Cooking Time | Serving

20 min   2

- Salad:
- 1 large broccoli stem, peeled and shredded
- 1/4 celery root bulb, peeled and shredded
- 1/8 cup chopped fresh Italian parsley
- 1/2 large beet, peeled and shredded
- 1 carrot, peeled and shredded
- 1/2 small red onion, sliced thin
- 1 zucchini, shredded
- Dressing:
- 1/2 teaspoon Dijon mustard
- 1/4 cup apple cider vinegar
- 1/2 tablespoon raw honey
- 1/2 teaspoon sea salt
- 1/8 teaspoon freshly ground black pepper
- 1 tablespoon extra-virgin olive oil
- Topping:

Dressing:
Mix all the ingredients in a small bowl

Salad:
oss all the ingredients in a large bowl.
Combine the ingredients for the dressing
small bowl, then stir to mix well

Soup with Roasted Vegetables

Cooking Time | Serving

45 min   3

- 1 parsnip, peeled and sliced
- 1 carrot, peeled and sliced
- 1 sweet potato, peeled and sliced
- 1/2 teaspoon chopped fresh rosemary
- 1/2 teaspoon chopped fresh thyme
- 1/2 teaspoon sea salt
- 1/4 teaspoon freshly ground black pepper
- 1 tablespoon extra-virgin olive oil
- 2 cups low-sodium vegetable soup
- 1/4 cup grated Parmesan cheese, for garnish (optional)

Preheat the oven to 400ºF.
Mix the parsnips, carrots, and sweet potatoes in a bowl,
Season it sprinkling with rosemary, thyme, salt, pepper, and olive oil.
Toss the vegetables to coat them properly
Learn the vegetables on a baking sheet with aluminium foil,
Let them roast in the oven for 30 minutes until soft
Flip the vegetables halfway through the roasting time.
Put the roasted vegetables with stock in a food processor or a mixer, then pulse until smooth.
Once the purée is ready warm it over low heat for 5 minutes.
gently pour the soup into a large serving bowl,
Scatter with Parmesan cheese.
Serve immediately.
Enjoy

Calories	Protein	Fat	Carbs	Fiber	Sodium
193	4.3g	5.5g	35.5g	5.2g	796mg

Balsamic Honey Salad

Cooking Time | Serving

15 min   4

1/2 cup balsamic vinegar
1/2 cup olive oil
2 tablespoon honey
2 teaspoon Dijon mustard
1/2 teaspoon garlic powder
1/2 teaspoon salt, or more to taste
Pinch freshly ground black pepper
Salad:
8 cups chopped red leaf lettuce
1 cup cherry or grape tomatoes, halved
1 English cucumber, sliced in quarters lengthwise and then cut into bite-size pieces
Any combination of fresh, torn herbs (parsley, oregano, basil, or chives)
2 tablespoon roasted sunflower seeds

Dressing
Combine the ingredient in a jar with a lid. Shake well.
Take a big jar with a lid, and make sure it can be sealed well
Mix in the jar
Shake energetically
Salad
Mix the lettuce, tomatoes, cucumber, and herbs in a medium bowl.
pour dressing at taste over the salad and mix them well
Top with sunflower seeds
serve and enjoy.

Calories	Protein	Fat	Carbs	Fiber	Sodium
347	4.8g	27.1g	22.9g	3.4g	178mg

Breakfast Recipes

Apple Omelet

Cooking Time | Serving

20 min   2

- 2 tablespoons all-purpose flour
- 1/6 teaspoon baking powder
- 1/8 teaspoon salt
- 2 to 3 large eggs, separated
- 2 tablespoons 2% milk
- 2/3 tablespoon lemon juice
- 2 tablespoons sugar
- 2/3 peeled and thinly sliced large apple
- 2/3 teaspoon sugar
- 1/6 teaspoon ground cinnamon

Heat your oven to about 375°. Combine the flour, baking powder, and salt. In a bowl, mix the egg yolks, milk, and lemon juice and stir them into the flour mixture.

In a medium bowl, beat the egg whites on medium speed until foamy; then gradually drizzle in the sugar, 1 tablespoon at a time; then fold into the flour mixture.

Pour the batter into a deep cake pan, about 9 inches, with cooking spray.

Place the apple slices directly on the deep pan; then add the sugar and the cinnamon.

Sprinkle on the plate coated with cooking spray. Place the apple slices on top. Mix the sugar and cinnamon and sprinkle over the apples.

Bake the cake, covered, for about 18 to 20 minutes; then enjoy!

Calories | Protein | Fat | Carbs |

253   11   5   10

Blueberry Breakfast Bowl

Cooking Time | Serving

20 min   2

2 cups fresh blueberries
2 cups fresh halved strawberries
1/2 teaspoon pure maple syrup
1/2 teaspoons almond flour
2/3 cup softened dates
2/3 cup raw walnuts
1/5 cup almond flour
1/3 teaspoon pure vanilla extract

Preheat your oven to a temperature of 180℃

Make the topping by mixing the dates in a food processor with walnuts, almond flour, and vanilla—a process at high speed.

Place the fresh berries on a baking sheet and mix with the almond flour and 2 teaspoons of maple syrup.

Sprinkle the crumbs of the topping over the berries, then cover your baking sheet with aluminum foil

Bake your breakfast for precisely 9 minutes

Remove the aluminum foil paper and bake for 15 more minutes.

Take the sheet out of the oven and let it cool for 5 minutes. Enjoy your breakfast!

Matcha Tea Latte

Cooking Time | Serving

5 min   2

- ¼ cup boiling water
- 1½ teaspoons matcha tea powder
- 1 cup of low-fat milk
- 1 teaspoon of honey

To make a fantastic matcha tea latte, mix the boiling water with the powder in a blender until foamy. Now heat the milk with the honey until it comes to a boil.

Mix the milk vigorously and pour it into a cup, then combine with the tea and enjoy.

Calories | Protein | Fat | Carbs | Sugar |

Calories	Protein	Fat	Carbs	Sugar
130	9.1g	3g	18.9g	18.4g

Turkish Mi

Cooking Time | Serving

8 min   2

- 1 cup sugar-free almond milk.
- 1 tablespoon fresh grated turmeric
- 2 teaspoons pure maple syrup or honey
- 1 teaspoon ginger
- Pinch of ground pepper
- 1 pinch of ground cinnamon for garnish

To make tasty Turkish-style milk, combine the milk, m syrup (or honey), turmeric, ginger, and pepper and m a blender.

Now pour into a small saucepan and allow to heat. place in a cup and garnish with cinnamon.

Calories | Protein | Fat | Carbs | Fiber | Sug

Calories	Protein	Fat	Carbs	Fiber	Sug
72	1.4g	2.7g	12g	1.1g	9g

Scrambled Eggs with Cabbage

Cooking Time | Serving

20 min   2

- Extra virgin olive oil
- 1 teaspoon Garlic
- 2 eggs
- 1 kale
- 1 teaspoon turmeric
- 1 teaspoon cayenne

Heat a skillet with a bit of oil to enjoy scrambled eggs with kale. Crack the eggs and cook them until scrambled. Now add the previously sliced or diced kale, cayenne, and turmeric.
Taste and enjoy.

weet Vegetable Smoothie

Cooking Time | Serving

5 min   2

1/3 bowl of red cabbage leaves
¾ cup freshly made apple juice (if from the supermarket that is 100% fruit)
1 bowl of diced pineapple
1/2 bowl of green grapes
1/2 bowl of chopped apple

To enjoy a great smoothie, combine the pineapple, apple juice, apple, and grapes in a blender. Blend everything. Now add the kale and mix again.
Now the smoothie is ready to be served and enjoyed.

alories	Protein	Fat	Carbs	Fiber
89	2.1g	1g	18g	283

Veg Rolls with Guacamole and Cauliflower

Cooking Time | Serving
30 min   2

- 1 kg cauliflower
- 120 g fat-free cheese
- 2 eggs
- 1/2 tsp. lemon zest
- 1/4 tsp. salt
- 120 g guacamole
- 120 g bell pepper (diced)
- 120 g tomato (diced)
- 120 g cucumber (diced)
- 1/4 onion (diced)
- 4 cabbage leaves

To cook fantastic veg rolls, preheat the form to 185°C (370° F).
Blend the cauliflower until small grains form.
Now cook the cauliflower in the microwave for about 4 minutes. Stir and recook for another 2 minutes.
Let cool, and squeeze into cloth to remove excess liquid.
Add the eggs, lemon zest, and salt to a bowl and mix until smooth.
Pour a small portion of the mixture onto a baking sheet lined with lightly greased baking paper. Using a spatula, distribute evenly until you have four medium-sized piadinas.
Bake for about 8 to 10 minutes, then flip and bake for another 5 to 7
Minutes. Carefully peel the wrappers off the baking paper and set them aside.
Now prepare the rolls by spreading the guacamole evenly over each wrap, garnishing with a cabbage leaf, dividing the remaining vegetables evenly between each wrap, then roll them up.

Calories | Protein | Fat | Carbs |
220   18.5   11.36g   13.2g

Breakfast with Mashed Cauliflow

Cooking Time | Serving
28 min   2

- 1 head of cauliflower
- 2 cloves of garlic, minced
- 1 tablespoon extra virgin olive oil
- ½ teaspoon salt
- 1 teaspoon ground black pepper
- Olive oil
- Chopped fresh thyme
- 1 pinch of salt

To enjoy this great breakfast, place a pot fu
salted water on medium heat.
Shred the cauliflower and set it aside.
Add the garlic and cauliflower to the water
cook for about 10 minutes.
Drain the cauliflower and set it aside in a b
for another 5 minutes.
Now put the garlic, cauliflower, salt, and pep
in a blender and blend until pureed.
Plate and enjoy.

Calories | Protein | Fat | Car
95   5.2g   5.1g   11g

Coconut and Green Apple Porridge

Cooking Time | Serving

6 min   3

- 2 tablespoons dried coconut
- 2 tablespoons toasted almonds
- ¼ cup of freezing water
- 1 cup of milk
- 2 tablespoons chia seeds
- ½ sizeable green apple, unpeeled and grated
- 5 strawberries, cut in half
- 1 cup low-fat yogurt (coconut if possible)

To make fantastic oatmeal, add half a cup of water to the chia seeds in a medium-sized bowl and stir; then set the mixture aside for a few minutes.

Meanwhile, prepare the rest of the ingredients. Add the grated apple, almonds, coconut, chia seeds, chopped strawberries, and milk. Stir vigorously and set aside for about 2 minutes. Add almond milk if needed or if the mixture is too thick.

Now serve the porridge in bowls and top with chopped strawberries and coconut yogurt.

Calories | Protein | Fat | Carbs |

131   3g   5g   11g

Breakfast with Quinoa and Raisins

Cooking Time | Serving

26 min   4

1 cup of quinoa
1 pinch of salt
2 ½ cups of water
4 cups almond milk
Anti-inflammatory cookbook for beginners 129
1 teaspoon vanilla extract
2/3 cup raisins
1 teaspoon cinnamon

To cook this sweet and healthy breakfast, rinse quinoa very well, drain and season with water and salt.

Cook the quinoa for about 20 minutes over medium-low heat. As soon as it becomes soft, add the almond milk.

Add the raisins and cinnamon and let it simmer for another 20 minutes, stirring often. As soon as it has absorbed the milk and gained consistency, remove it from the heat and add the vanilla.

Taste and enjoy

Calories | Protein | Fat | Carbs |

162   6g   7.4g   21g

Eggs with Zucchini Noodles

Cooking Time | Serving

22 min   2

- 2 tablespoons extra-virgin olive oil
- 4 zucchinis
- 4 eggs
- Salt and black pepper to the taste
- 1 tablespoon basil

To enjoy this fantastic recipe, place zucchini noodles in a bowl with salt, pepper, and olive oil and toss well.

Take a baking sheet and grease it. Now arrange the zucchini noodles into 4 portions on the baking sheet.

Crack an egg over each piece, add salt and pepper and bake at 350°F (about 180°C) for 11 minutes in a ventilated oven.

Serve when ready and enjoy.

Calories | Protein | Fat | Carbs | Fiber |

301   15.1g   27.6g   11.7g   4.1g

Oats with Banana and Da

Cooking Time | Serving

15 min   2

- 1 banana, peeled and sliced
- 1 of a cup of almond milk
- ½ cup iced coffee
- 2 pitted dates
- 1 tablespoon cocoa powder
- 1 cup of oats

To prepare this fantastic dish, put everythin a blender. Combine the banana with the and the rest of the ingredients, blend, di into bowls and serve for breakfast.

Calories | Protein | Fat | Carbs | Fib

460   9.3g   26.1g   56.2g   12

Vegan Bowl with Hummus and Avocado

Cooking Time | Serving

12 min   6

- 1 tablespoon olive oil
- 1 pound of cut asparagus (without the white part)
- 4 cups kale, shredded
- 3 cups Brussels sprouts
- ½ cup hummus
- 1 avocado, peeled, pitted, and sliced
- 4 eggs alone, peeled and sliced
- For the dressing:
- 2 tablespoons olive oil
- Salt and black pepper to taste

To prepare this fantastic bowl, heat a skillet with 2 tablespoons of oil over medium-high heat, add asparagus, and saute for 5 minutes, stirring often.

Now take a salad bowl, combine the asparagus with the cabbage, hummus, avocado, and eggs and toss gently.

Add the dressing, toss, and enjoy.

Calories | Fat | Carbs | Fiber |

352   22g   24.2g   10.7g

uit and Vegetable Smoothie

Cooking Time | Serving

5 min   2

3 1/2 cups spinach
1 green apple, pitted and diced
1 avocado peeled, pitted, and diced
3 tablespoons chia seeds
1 teaspoon honey
1 frozen banana cut into cubes
2 cups coconut water (coconut infused in the cups of water for about 2 hours)

We take a blender and combine all the ingredients, blend vigorously until smooth and without lumps.

We put them into glasses and enjoy this healthy breakfast.

lories | Protein | Fat | Carbs | Fiber |

175   2.1g   11.1g   23g   8g

Salty Muffin

Cooking Time | Serving

40 min   12

- 1 cup quinoa, cooked
- 5 beaten eggs prepared previously
- Salt and black pepper to taste
- 1 small yellow onion, chopped
- 1 ½ cups white mushrooms, sliced
- ½ cup sun-dried tomatoes

To prepare a savory muffin, take a bowl and combine the eggs with all the ingredients, and beat well until you get a nice mixture.

Import everything into a silicone muffin pan, bake at 350°F (180°C) for about 30 minutes and serve.

Calories | Protein | Fat | Carbs | Fiber |

132   8.1g   5.8g   12.8g   1.3g

Ome

Cooking Time | Serving

37 min   5

- 1 teaspoon olive oil
- 1 red onion, diced
- 1 sweet potato, diced
- 1 diced green bell pepper
- 1 clove of garlic, minced
- 1 cup chopped white mushrooms
- ½ cup of quinoa
- 1 cup chicken broth
- 4 eggs, beaten
- Salt and black pepper to taste

To make a tasty omelet, heat a skillet with over medium-low heat, add the onion, ga peppers, sweet potato, and mushrooms, saute for 5 minutes.

Add the quinoa, stir, and cook for ano minute.

Add the broth, salt, and pepper, stir and c for 15 minutes.

Divide the mixture among plates, top e serving with a fried egg, sprinkle with salt pepper, and serve for breakfast.

Calories | Protein | Fat | Carbs | Fib

311   17.8   14   32   3.

Ham Muffins

Cooking Time | Serving

27 min   4

- 10 slices of ham
- 5 eggs previously beaten
- 1/2 cup frozen, chopped spinach
- ¼ cup feta cheese, crumbled
- A pinch of salt and black pepper
- 1 1/2 tablespoons basil pesto

To cook these fantastic ham muffins, grease a muffin pan with oil and line each mold with 1 1/2 slices of ham.

Mix the pesto eggs, salt, and pepper in a separate bowl and pour into the molds with the ham.

We bake the muffins in the oven at 400 degrees F° (190°C) for 15 minutes and serve them for breakfast.

Calories	Protein	Fat	Carbs	Fiber
121	10	7.1	2.1	1.8

anana Quinoa and Clove Mix

Cooking Time | Serving

2 hours   10

4 cups bananas, peeled and mashed
1/2 cup maple syrup
1/3 cup molasses
1 tablespoon cinnamon powder
2 teaspoons vanilla extract
1/2 teaspoon finely ground cloves
½ teaspoon ground ginger
1 cup of quinoa
¼ cup ground almonds
2 ½ cups almond milk

To enjoy this fantastic dish, take a baking dish and combine the bananas with maple syrup, molasses, and all the other ingredients. Mix and bake at 350° F (190°C) in a fan-assisted oven for about 1 hour and 30 minutes.

Check occasionally so that nothing in the oven burns. As soon as baked, take it out, cut it, and enjoy it for breakfast.

Calories	Protein	Fat	Carbs	Fiber
220	4.9	5.1	42	5

Bowl of Chickpeas Tomatoes and Green Olives

Cooking Time | Serving

45 min   5

- 14 ounces (400gr) canned chickpeas, drained and rinsed
- 1/3 teaspoon cardamom, ground
- ½ teaspoon cinnamon powder
- 1 teaspoon turmeric powder
- 1 teaspoon ground coriander
- 1 tablespoon olive oil
- A pinch of salt and black pepper
- ¾ cup Greek yogurt
- ½ cup pitted and diced green olives
- ½ cup diced cherry tomatoes
- 1 and a half thinly sliced cucumbers

Spread the chickpeas on a lined baking sheet to cook this fantastic dish. Add the spices, oil, salt, and pepper. Mix everything well and bake at 370°F for about 30 minutes.

Next, combine the roasted chickpeas with the rest of the ingredients, mix and enjoy for breakfast.

Calories | Protein | Fat | Carbs | Fiber |

Calories	Protein	Fat	Carbs	Fiber
220	4.9	4.1	47	5

Tuna Sal

Cooking Time | Serving

10 min   3

- 13 ounces canned tuna in water, drained and without oil
- 1/2 cup roasted red peppers, chopped
- 1 tablespoon capers
- 8 olives, pitted and sliced
- 1 tablespoon olive oil
- 1 teaspoon chopped parsley
- 1 teaspoon lemon juice
- A pinch of salt and black pepper

To prepare this great tuna breakfast, tak bowl, and combine the tuna with the roas peppers and the rest of the ingredients.
Mix well to get an excellent distribution of ingredients.
Enjoy breakfast.

Calories | Protein | Fat | Carbs | Fib

Calories	Protein	Fat	Carbs	Fib
255	12.1	19.3	3.7	0.

Vegetarian Savory Pie

Cooking Time | Serving

2 hours   10

- 1 cup of sun-dried tomatoes
- 1 prepared pie crust
- 2 tablespoons almond oil
- 1 diced yellow onion
- 1 clove of garlic chopped
- 1 red bell pepper, chopped
- ¼ cup green (or black) olives, pitted and sliced
- 1 teaspoon parsley
- 1 teaspoon oregano
- 1/2 cup feta cheese, crumbled
- 4 eggs, beaten
- 1 ½ cups almond milk
- Salt and black pepper to taste

To prepare this fantastic savory pie, heat a skillet with oil over medium-high heat.

Add garlic and onion and sauté for about 4 minutes.

Add the olives, parsley, spinach, oregano, salt, and pepper and cook for another 5 minutes.

Add the tomatoes and stir while removing from the heat.

Now place the back crust in a cake pan. Pour all the contents inside and spread well.

Mix the eggs with salt, pepper, milk, and half the cheese separately, and beat and pour the mixture into the crust.

Sprinkle the remaining cheese over the top and bake at 375 degrees for 40 minutes.

Let the pie cool, cut into slices, and serve for breakfast.

Calories	Protein	Fat	Carbs
220	8.6	1.4	13

owl Of Corn Shrimp and Cherry Tomatoes

Cooking Time | Serving

24 min   4

2 packages of canned corn, drained
1 avocado, peeled, pitted, and chopped
8 leaves of chopped basil
A pinch of salt and black pepper
1 kg shrimp, shelled and lightly blanched
1 and ½ cups cherry tomatoes, cut in half
2 teaspoons of olive oil

To enjoy this energy-filled breakfast, thread the shrimp onto skewers and brush with a bit of oil. Place skewers on the preheated grill, cook over medium heat for 3 minutes on each side and remove skewers.

Add the rest of the ingredients to the bowl, mix, divide among plates, and serve for breakfast.

lories	Protein	Fat	Carbs	Fiber
380	30	24	29	7

Tomato Lentil and Yogurt Salad

Cooking Time | Serving

70 min   5

- 2 finely chopped onions
- 2 cloves of garlic, minced
- 2 cups already rinsed lentils.
- 1 tablespoon olive oil
- A pinch of salt and black pepper
- ½ teaspoon sweet paprika
- 3 cups of water
- ¼ cup of lemon juice
- ¾ cup Greek yogurt
- 2 tablespoons of tomato paste

To prepare this tasty dish, heat a pot with oil over medium-high heat, and add the onions and sauté for about 3 minutes.

Add the garlic and lentils, stir and cook for 1 minute more.

Now you need to add the 3 cups of water, bring it to a boil and cook covered for 30 minutes.

Add lemon juice and remaining ingredients except for yogurt.

Stir everything together, divide the mixture into bowls, top with yogurt and eat.

Calories | Protein | Fat | Carbs | Fiber |

Calories	Protein	Fat	Carbs	Fiber
294	21	3	49	8

Pan Fried Zucchini and Quin

Cooking Time | Serving

30 min   4

- 1 tablespoon olive oil
- 1 clove of garlic, finely chopped
- 1 cup of quinoa
- 1 zucchini, diced
- 5 basil leaves, finely chopped
- ¼ cup green olives, pitted and chopped
- 1 tomato, diced
- ½ cup feta cheese, crumbled
- 2 cups water
- 1 cup canned chickpeas, drained and rinsed
- A pinch of salt and black pepper

To prepare this fantastic and tasty recipe, ▊ a skillet with oil over medium-high heat, ▊ the garlic and quinoa, and sauté for abo▊ minutes.

Next step, add the water, zucchini, salt, ▊ pepper, stir, bring to a boil and cook for a▊ 18 minutes.

Add the rest of the ingredients, stir, divide ▊ plates and eat.

Calories | Protein | Fat | Carbs | Fib

Calories	Protein	Fat	Carbs	Fib
300	13	12	45	8

Brown Rice Salad

Cooking Time | Serving

10 min   4

- 8 ounces (220 g) of previously cooked brown rice
- 7 cups arugula
- 13 ounces (370 gr.) canned chickpeas, drained and rinsed
- 4 ounces (110 gr.) feta cheese, crumbled
- ¾ cup basil, chopped
- A pinch of salt and black pepper
- 2 tablespoons lemon juice
- ¼ teaspoon lemon zest, grated
- ¼ cup olive oil

To prepare this fantastic rice salad dish, combine all the ingredients inside a bowl.
Add the previously cooked rice to the rest of the ingredients to make a smooth mixture.
Enjoy

Calories	Protein	Fat	Carbs	Fiber
510	11	24	55	7.3

Quinoa with Walnuts and Blueberries

Cooking Time | Serving

8 min   3

1 cup blueberries
¼ cup walnuts, chopped
2 cups almond milk
½ teaspoon cinnamon powder
2 cups of already cooked quinoa
1 tablespoon honey

Put the quinoa, milk, and other ingredients in a bowl to enjoy this fantastic fit dish. Mix and divide into smaller bowls to serve for breakfast. Enjoy

Calories	Protein	Fat	Carbs	Fiber
312	4.4	15.1	16.4	3.6

Carrot Cake

Cooking Time | Serving

60 min   6

- 1/4 cup coconut oil, at room temperature, plus more for greasing the baking dish
- 1 teaspoon pure vanilla extract
- 1/8 cup pure maple syrup 6 eggs
- 1/4 cup olive flour
- 1/2 teaspoon baking powder
- 1/2 teaspoon baking soda
- 1/4 teaspoon ground nutmeg
- 1/2 teaspoon ground cinnamon
- 1/2 teaspoon sea salt
- 1/4 cup chopped pecans
- 2 cups finely grated carrots

Prepare the oven by heating it to 350ºF. Grease a 13x9-inch baking dish with olive oil.

In a large bowl, stir the vanilla extract, maple syrup, and ½ cup of olive oil to mix them well

Break the eggs in the same bowl and whisk.

In a separate bowl, mix the coconut flour, baking powder, baking soda, nutmeg, cinnamon, and salt

Combine the eggs with the flour mixture

Add the pecans and carrots to the bowl and mix them using a spoon

Pour the mixture into the baking dish.

Bake for 45 minutes (the cake spring back when lightly pressed with your fingers once ready)

Let it rest for 15 minutes.

Serve and enjoy

Calories | Protein | Fat | Carbs | Fiber | Sodium |

Calories	Protein	Fat	Carbs	Fiber	Sodium
253	5.5	21.4	2.3	12.2	205

Kefir and Berries Oa

Cooking Time | Serving

30 min   2

- For the oats:
- 1/2 cup steel-cut oats (look for certified gluten-free if you have a gluten intolerance)
- 1 1/2 cups water
- pinch of salt
- For topping (these are all optional and to-taste):
- fresh or frozen fruit/berries
- a handful of sliced almonds, pepitas, hemp seeds, or other nuts/seed
- unsweetened kefir
- drizzle of maple syrup or a sprinkling of coconut sugar to taste

Toast the oats in a saucepan over medium h stirring for 2 minutes.

Add the water and bring to a boil.

Reduce the heat to a simmer, and cook about 25 minutes; check for the tenderness like before serving

Serve with a handful of berries and se a bunch of kefir, and the sweetener of y choice.

Enjoy

Chia Seeds Porridge

Cooking Time | Serving

30 min   3-4

- 1/2 cup buckwheat, rinsed
- 1/4 cup oats
- 1 tablespoon chia seeds
- 1 cups milk (cow's, almond, or soy)
- 1 cups water
- 1/2 each pear and apple, grated with skin on
- 1/2 teaspoon each ground ginger and cinnamon
- 1/4 teaspoon each ground nutmeg and cardamom
- 1 tablespoons nut butter
- 1/2 teaspoon vanilla extract
- 1 tablespoon honey

Mixed Barry Compote
- 250 grams of mixed frozen berries
- finely grated zest and juice 1 orange
- 1/6 cup caster sugar
- 1 teaspoons cornflour
- 1/2 tablespoon water

Immerse the buckwheat and oats in cold water
In a separate bowl, immerse chia seeds in a cup of milk.
3. Leave both bowls on the bench to soak overnight.
4. Drain the buckwheat and oats in a fine sieve, then rinse well under cold water.
5. In a saucepan, place the chia seeds, 1 more cup of milk, buckwheat and oats, water, grated pear and apple, all the spices, nut butter, vanilla, and honey. Cook for 30 minutes, often stirring, until creamy (add more water or milk to keep the consistency if needed)
Top with your choice.
Serve in bowls and enjoy

Mixed Barry Compote

Slowly bring to the boil the berries, the orange zest and juice, and the caster sugar in a saucepan.
Combine the cornflour and water in a bowl until smooth, then stir into the berries.
Simmer for a couple of minutes.
Use as topping for porridge.

Blueberry Gluten Free Pancakes

Cooking Time | Serving

30 min   16

2 large eggs, room temperature
2 1/2 cups buttermilk
1/2 cup Chobani plain, non-fat yogurt
4 tablespoons brown sugar
2 tablespoon olive oil
1 teaspoon vanilla extract
2 cups plus 4 tablespoons buckwheat flour
3 teaspoons baking powder
1/2 teaspoon cinnamon
1 teaspoon salt
4 cups fresh blueberries

Heat a large pan on medium heat.
Mix eggs, buttermilk, yogurt, brown sugar, olive oil, and vanilla extract, whisking in a big bowl.
Whisk together buckwheat flour, baking powder, cinnamon, and salt together separate from the other ingredients
Incorporate the two bowls, and stir until combined.
Preheat the grill (medium-low heat). Once it is hot, grease with oil per each pancake, pour ¼ cup of batter onto the surface, then sprinkle with blueberries.
Cook on the side until holes form around the edges, then flip the repeat on the other side.
Serve with blueberries, nuts, and maple syrup!

Special Scrambled Eggs

Cooking Time | Serving

20   2

- 6 free-range or organic eggs
- 2 teaspoon fresh grated turmeric (see notes)
- 2 teaspoon chia seeds
- 4 tablespoons organic coconut milk or cream
- Pinch sea salt
- 4 teaspoons cold pressed olive oil
- 200 g baby spinach leaves
- 2 tablespoon Basil Pesto

Mix eggs, chia turmeric, sea salt, and coconut milk in a small bowl. Whisk until homogeneous, then set aside.

Heat 1 teaspoon olive oil in a pan over low heat. Add the spinach and cook for 30 seconds

Remove the spinach and pour in the egg mixture; stir using a wooden spoon until the eggs become soft and creamy

Add the spinach and fold

Serve with pesto

Poached egg - Avocado - Salmon Toɑ

Cooking Time | Serving

14 min   2

- Soy sauce and sesame seeds.
- 4 slices of bread, toasted
- 1 large avocado, smashed
- 1/2 tsp freshly squeezed lemon juice
- Pinch of kosher salt and cracked black pepper
- 7 oz smoked salmon
- 4 eggs, poached
- Splash of Kikkoman soy sauce, optional
- 2 Tbsp thinly sliced scallions
- Microgreens, optional

Make the avocado dressing by smashing the avoc in a small bowl and adding lemon juice and a p of salt. Then set aside

Poach your eggs. In a small pot, bring water boil, then low down the heat and add a teaspoo vinegar to the water.

Break one egg in a small bowl or a cup using a sp make a vortex in hot water and vinegar mixture, gently pour your egg from the bowl inside the w

Let it cook for exactly 2 minutes without touchir

Use a spoon or a skimmer to remove the egg the water and set it aside; repeat for each egg.

Make the toast

Toast your bread.

Spread the avocado on one side of the bread add the salmon.

Carefully transfer the poached eggs onto the sa toasts.

Pour a splash of soy sauce and some cracked pe and garnish with scallions and microgreens.

Enjoy!

Yogurt Berries and Nuts Parfait

Cooking Time | Serving

10 min   4

- 4 tablespoons honey
- 3 cups unsweetened plain coconut yogurt or plain unsweetened yogurt or almond yogurt
- 2 cups of fresh blueberries
- 1/2 cup of walnut pieces
- 1 cup of fresh raspberries

Mix the yogurt and honey.
Divide into two bowls.
Sprinkle blueberries and raspberries together with 60g chopped walnuts

Calories	Protein	Fat	Carbs	Fiber	Sodium	Sugar
503	22g	25	56.1g	8g	172mg	45.2

atmeal and Cinnamon with Dried Blueberries

Cooking Time | Serving

10 min   4

2 cups of almond milk
2 cups of oats
2 teaspoons ground cinnamon
2 cups water
1 pinch of sea salt
1 cup dried blueberries

Bring the almond milk, salt, and water to a medium saucepan.
Add the blueberries, oats, and cinnamon.
Reduce heat and stir for 5 minutes.
Remove the oats from the heat. Allow to repostage the pot for 3 minutes.
Stir before serving.
Serve and enjoy!

alories	Protein	Fat	Carbs	Fiber	Sodium	Sugar
504	25g	25	51g	9g	173mg	42g

Chia Based Breakfast Pudding

Cooking Time | Serving

60 min   4

- 1 cup chia seeds
- 1 teaspoon vanilla extract
- 1 cup chopped cashews, divided
- 2 cups almond milk
- 1/2 cup maple syrup OR honey
- 1 cup sugarfree pitted cherries frozen, thawed, with juice reserve, split

Combine chia seeds, man- milk, mandorla, maple syrup, and vanilla in a four container with an airtight closure.

Set aside after shaking well, and let stand at least one hour.

Pour the pudding into two bowls and finish with a quarter cup of cherries and two tablespoons of cashews.

Calories	Protein	Fat	Carbs	Fiber	Sodium	Sugar
272	6g	14g	38g	6g	84mg	25g

Coconut Rice with Berr

Cooking Time | Serving

40 min   4

- 80 ml of water
- 3/4 teaspoon salt
- 120 g fresh blueberries or raspberries, divided
- 120 g flaked coconut, divided
- 120 g brown basmati rice
- 120 ml coconut milk
- 2 pitted and chopped dates
- 60 g toasted almonds, split

Combine the water, basmati rice, coconut coconut, spices, and date pieces in a med saucepan over high heat.

Stir constantly until the mixture boils. Turn heat to minimal and cook, stirring occasion Occasionally, for 20 to 30 minutes, OR until rice is tender.

Place a few blueberries, almonds, and CO on each serving of rice.

Calories	Protein	Fat	Carbs	Fiber	Sodium	Sug
281	6g	8g	49g	5g	623mg	7g

Apple Jam

Cooking Time | Serving

25 min 8

- 12 apples
- 1/2 cup raw honey
- 2 teaspoon ground cinnamon
- 1/2 cup apple juice
- Sea salt, to taste

Peel the apples, core and finely chop them

Put the chopped apples and the rest of the ingredients in a stockpot.

Carefully combine them, then cook over medium-high heat for 10 minutes constantly stirring.

Serve immediately with a slice of bread.

Calories | Protein | Fat | Carbs | Fiber | Sodium |

Calories	Protein	Fat	Carbs	Fiber	Sodium
243	1.5g	0.4g	66.2g	9.2g	64mg

Peanut Butter and Chocolate Cold Snacks

Cooking Time | Serving

45 min 30

2 cup creamy peanut butter
1/2 cup unsweetened cocoa powder
4 tablespoons softened almond butter
1 teaspoon vanilla extract
3 1/2 cups maple syrup

Line a big plate or a baking with greaseproof paper.

Combine all the ingredients, mixing them in a big bowl

Divide the mixture into 30 parts and shape them into as many balls (1 inch wide).

Arrange the balls on the paper and refrigerate for at least 1h, then serve chilled.

Calories | Protein | Fat | Carbs | Fiber | Sodium|

Calories	Protein	Fat	Carbs	Fiber	Sodium
143	4.4g	8.4g	16.5g	1.2g	75mg

Fruits & Desserts

Amazing Berry Almond Smoothie

Cooking Time | Serving

10 min   1-2

- 2/3 cup fresh raspberries
- ½ cup blueberries
- 2 frozen and chopped bananas
- ½ cup plain almond milk with a pinch of salt
- 5 and ½ tablespoons chopped almonds
- ¼ teaspoon cinnamon
- ½ teaspoon vanilla extract
- 1 tablespoon coconut powder

In order to enjoy a delicious Smoothie, blend all ingredients in a blender until smooth.

Pour the smoothie into a bowl and enjoy it after storage for at least 20 minutes in the freezer.

Calories	Protein	Fat	Carbs	Sugar
310	10g	19g	39.9g	21.4

iced Pecans Nuts

Cooking Time | Serving

1 hour 20 min   15-20

5 cups pecans
1 egg white
1 tablespoon water
6 tablespoons of sugar
½ teaspoon salt
¼ teaspoon finely chopped cloves
¼ teaspoon nutmeg
a pinch of ground cinnamon
a Pinch of cayenne pepper

To enjoy this fantastic dish, preheat the ventilated oven to 270 degrees F. Apply baking paper to a baking sheet and set aside.

In a bowl, set aside, combine all the ingredients (except for the walnuts) and mix in order to get the egg whites to blend with everything else.

Add the pecans and mix to coat them evenly. Spread in a single layer on the prepared baking sheet.

Allow cooling completely on the baking sheet, about 20 minutes. Break into pieces before serving.

Calories	Protein	Fat	Carbs	Fiber	Sodium
162	2.1g	15.6g	6.9g	283	5.4g

Camomile Based Regenerate

Cooking Time | Serving

20 min   4-6

- 5 cups of boiling water
- 7 sachets of chamomile tea
- 2 1/2 teaspoons freshly grated ginger
- 4 lemon slices
- 4 teaspoons honey
- 2 sprigs of lightly chopped rosemary

To create a warm, tonic chamomile infusion, pour the cups of boiling water into a large pot. Now add the chamomile tea and let it sit for about 8 minutes.

When the minutes are up, add all the rest of the ingredients and, using a spoon, stir gently. Serve with a freshly infused rosemary leaf.

Calories | Protein | Sugar | Carbs |

8   0.2g   4g   1.1

Carrot Energy Ba

Cooking Time | Serving

18 min   20

- 1 cup previously pitted dates
- ½ cup of oats
- ¼ cup chopped pecans
- ¼ cup chia seeds
- 2 medium carrots, finely chopped
- 1 teaspoon vanilla extract
- ¾ teaspoon ground cinnamon
- ½ teaspoon ground ginger
- ¼ teaspoon ground turmeric
- ¼ teaspoon salt
- Pinch of ground pepper

In order to make your own fantastic ca energy bars, combine the dates, nuts, seeds, and oats in a blender and blend u smooth.

When everything is smooth, add the var carrots, and all the other ingredients. N form them into bars and store them in refrigerator.

After a few hours, enjoy them!

Calories | Protein | Fat | Carbs | Fiber | Sodiu

52   0.7g   1.3g   9.1g   1.9g   6g

Fruit Smoothie and Matcha

Cooking Time | Serving

12 min   2

- ½ cup sliced banana
- ½ cup sliced peaches
- 1 cup fresh spinach
- ½ cup unsweetened almond milk
- 5 tablespoons chopped almonds, divided into.
- 1 ½ teaspoon matcha tea powder
- 1 teaspoon maple syrup
- ½ ripe kiwi fruit, diced

In order to make a fantastic matcha smoothie, blend the banana, peaches, spinach, almond milk, almonds matcha, and maple syrup in a blender until smooth. Then take the mixture and pour it into a bowl, then add the kiwifruit and the remaining 2 tablespoons of chopped almonds.
Serve and enjoy.

Calories	Protein	Fat	Carbs	Fiber	Sugar
420	10.1g	18.6g	44.8g	9.3g	27g

Almond Biscuits

Cooking Time | Serving

60 min   48 pieces

180 g all-purpose flour
¼ cup (30 g) ground flaxseed
¼ cup (50 g) sugar
½ cup (12 g) sugar substitute
2 teaspoons baking powder
½ teaspoon cinnamon
¼ cup (72 g) salt
88 g almonds, roughly chopped
3 egg whites
2 tablespoons (28 ml) plus 1 teaspoon (5 ml) of skimmed milk
2 tablespoons (28 ml) of canola oil
2 teaspoons (10 ml) of vanilla
Four to five 28 g squares of bittersweet chocolate are optional.

Preheat the oven to 356 °F, and line a baking tray with baking paper. Mix the flour, linseed, sugar, sugar substitute, baking powder, cinnamon, and salt in a large bowl.
Combine the almonds in a separate bowl, beat the egg whites, skim milk, canola oil, and vanilla, and add to the flour mixture. Knead lightly in the bowl and transfer to a floured surface; knead until smooth. Divide the dough in half to form two 20 cm long logs; place the logs on baking paper and press until they are 5 cm wide and 2.5 cm high; bake for 32 minutes. Slide the rolls and paper onto a wire rack and leave to cool for 30 minutes.
Heat the oven to 356 °F and line 2 baking trays with baking paper. Using a serrated knife, cut the biscuit logs diagonally into 1 cm wide slices. Place the slices cut side down on baking paper and bake another 10 minutes. (The second baking gives the biscuits their characteristic crispness.) Bake and allow to cool on the baking sheets.
For a special treat, coat one end of each biscuit with chocolate: break the chocolate into small squares and melt in a bain-marie, stirring often. Quickly dip the cooled biscuit ends into the chocolate and place them on baking paper until the chocolate has hardened.

Calories	Protein	Fat	Carbs
58	2g	3g	5g

Purple Fruit Mix

Cooking Time | Serving

20 min   6

- 2 cups pitted black grapes
- 2 cups cut cranberries
- 2 cups diced plums
- 1 tablespoon chopped basil

In order to make this fantastic recipe, combine all ingredients in a large bowl and mix with a spoon.
To give the dish more flavor, you can add yogurt if needed.
Enjoy your dish!

Calories | Protein | Fat | Carbs | Fiber | Sodium |

Calories	Protein	Fat	Carbs	Fiber	Sodium
56	0.7g	0.2g	14.6g	1.5g	11.4

Avocado Cherry and Spinach Smoot|

Cooking Time | Serving

5 min   1

- 1 cup plain low-fat kefir.
- 1 cup frozen cherries
- ½ cup of baby spinach leaves
- ¼ cup mashed ripe avocado
- 1 tablespoon of salted almond butter
- 1 piece of peeled ginger

To make this tasty smoothie, start by put the kefir in a blender and add all the remair ingredients (except the chia seeds). Blend you get a lump-free, smooth smoothie. Fir for garnish, add the chia seeds and enjoy.

Calories | Protein | Fat | Carbs | Fiber | Sug

Calories	Protein	Fat	Carbs	Fiber	Sug
56	0.7	0.2g	14.4g	1.5	11.

Fantastic Chia Seed and Cocoa Pudding

Cooking Time | Serving

18 min   2

- 2 tablespoons of chia seeds
- 460 ml of water
- 1 cup of chocolate whey protein (powdered)
- 1 Greek yogurt
- ½ cup flaxseed (optional but recommended)
- 1 tablespoon of bitter cocoa powder
- Stevia

To prepare this tasty pudding, start by mixing the chia seeds and let them sit in water for about 18 minutes. Remember to give it a stir every now and then.

After about 20 minutes, add all the other ingredients and stir vigorously. Let's leave everything together for about 30 minutes in the refrigerator before we can enjoy it.

Calories | Protein | Fat | Carbs |

Calories	Protein	Fat	Carbs
255	2.5	28	4.1

Maple Syrup and Cranberry Protein Bars

Cooking Time | Serving

55 min   15

2 tablespoons extra virgin olive oil
2 medium ripe bananas, mashed
½ cup sugar-free almond butter
½ cup maple syrup
1/3 cup cranberries
1 and ½ cups of oats
¼ cup of oatmeal
¼ cup ground flaxseed
¼ teaspoon ground cloves
2 teaspoons ground coconut
½ teaspoon ground cinnamon
1 teaspoon vanilla extract

To prepare tasty protein bars, preheat the oven to about 400°F (210°C). Take a baking pan and line it with baking paper, and sprinkle a little olive oil on the base of it.

Mash the bananas, add them to the almond butter and maple syrup and stir to mix well.

Then add to the other ingredients and mix until you get a smooth mixture.

Now arrange on the baking sheet and bake for 40 minutes.

Take out of the oven, cut, and shape into bars. Serve and enjoy.

Calories | Protein | Fat | Carbs | Fiber | Sodium |

Calories	Protein	Fat	Carbs	Fiber	Sodium
155	4g	8g	20g	2g	4mg

Cranberry and Quinoa Energy Bars

Cooking Time | Serving

20 min   15

- 2 tablespoons almond butter
- 2 tablespoons maple syrup
- ¾ cup of quinoa
- 1 tablespoon previously dried cranberries
- 1 tablespoon chia seeds
- ¼ cup ground almonds
- ¼ cup previously toasted sesame seeds
- 1 orange
- ½ teaspoon vanilla extract

To prepare these tasty energy bars, line a baking sheet with baking paper.

Combine butter with maple syrup in a bowl. Stir to mix well. Add remaining ingredients and stir until the mixture is smooth and completely lump-free.

Now you need to divide the resulting dough into 12 equal parts, shaping each part like a candy bar.

Arrange the bars on the baking sheet, then refrigerate for at least 15 minutes.

Serve and enjoy them.

Calories | Protein | Fat | Carbs | Fiber | Sodium |

Calories	Protein	Fat	Carbs	Fiber	Sodium
121	3.1g	11g	5.1g	3g	211mg

Tasty Berry Ta

Cooking Time | Serving

55 min   8

- **Tart:**
- 1 and 1/2 cups fresh raspberries
- 2 cups fresh blueberries
- Anti-inflammatory cookbook for beginners 160
- 1 cup sliced rhubarb pieces
- ¼ cup apple juice
- 2 tablespoons coconut oil
- ¼ cup honey
- **Garnish:**
- 1 cup almond flour
- ½ cup coconut mix
- ¼ cup honey
- ½ cup coconut oil

Preheat the oven to 180ºC (370°F).

Take a baking pan and grease it with me coconut oil.

Proceed to combine the ingredients in a l bowl. Stir and mix well.

Spread the mixture in a single layer on baking sheet. Set aside.

Now let's prepare the inner mixture.

We combine the almond flour and Coconut bowl. We proceed to stir to mix well.

We add the honey and Coconut oil and proc with a fork until the mixture is crumbled.

Bake in preheated oven for 35 minutes or golden brown.

Serve

Calories | Protein | Fat | Carbs | Fiber | Sodiu

Calories	Protein	Fat	Carbs	Fiber	Sodiu
310	3.5g	32.1g	29.8g	6g	3mg

Brown Rice with Blueberries and Coconut

Cooking Time | Serving

62 min   3

- 1 cup fresh blueberries
- 2 cups unsweetened coconut milk
- half teaspoon of ground ginger
- ¼ cup maple syrup
- Sea salt, to taste
- 2 cups of previously cooked brown rice

To enjoy this particular rice and forest fruit dish, place all ingredients except brown rice in a pot. Stir to combine well.

Now cook over medium-high heat for 7 minutes or until the blueberries are tender.

Now pour in the brown rice and cook for another 3 minutes or until the rice is soft.

Stir constantly.

Now enjoy!

Calories	Protein	Fat	Carbs	Fiber	Sodium
450	7g	24.8g	62g	5.0g	75mg

Blueberry and Crisp Oat Bars

Cooking Time | Serving

38 min   4

- 3 tablespoons coconut oil
- 5 cups fresh blueberries
- Juice half a lemon
- 2 teaspoons lemon zest
- 1 teaspoon maple syrup
- 1 cup gluten-free oats (if needed)
- 1 cup chopped pecans
- Salt to taste

To prepare these tasty bars, preheat the oven to 180°C (360°F). Grease a baking pan with a little coconut oil (set some aside, we will need it later).

In a bowl, combine the blueberries, lemon juice and zest, and maple syrup. We mix everything together and spread it on the baking sheet.

Combine the remaining ingredients in a small bowl. Stir to mix well. Pour the mixture over the blueberry mixture.

Bake in preheated oven for 20 minutes or until oats are golden brown.

Out of the oven, shape into a candy bar, and let cool. Let's eat and enjoy.

Calories	Protein	Fat	Carbs	Fiber	Sodium
500	5.1g	33g	51g	7g	41mg

Lemony & Blackberry Granita

Cooking Time | Serving

10 min   4

- 460 g fresh blackberries
- 1 teaspoon chopped fresh thyme
- ¼ cup squeezed lemon juice
- ½ cup honey
- ½ cup water

To prepare this fantastic dish, we put all the ingredients in a food processor and puree.

Pour the mixture through a sieve into a baking dish. Discard the seeds left in the sieve. We won't need them for later, so let's throw them away.

Place the dish in the freezer for about 2 hours. Remove from the freezer and stir to break up any frozen bits.

Return the dish to the freezer for 1 hour, then stir again to break up any frozen parts.

Return the dish to the freezer for 4 hours until the slush is completely frozen.

Remove from freezer and mash to serve.

Enjoy.

Calories | Protein | Fat | Carbs | Fiber | Sodium |

Calories	Protein	Fat	Carbs	Fiber	Sodium
190	2.2g	2.1g	47g	6g	7mg

Cold Mango and Coconut Ca...

Cooking Time | Serving

60 min   6

- Crust:
- 1 cup toasted cashews
- ½ cup oats
- 1 cup pitted dates
- Filling:
- 2 mangoes, peeled and cut into pieces
- ½ cup unsweetened shredded Coconut
- 1 cup coconut milk
- ½ cup of water

To prepare this tasty pie crust, we com[ ] the ingredients for the crust in a blender blend. We now pour the resulting mixture a baking pan and cover the bottom well.

We now put the ingredients for the pie fillin the blender and create a smooth puree.

We now pour the puree over the crust, usi spoon to distribute it evenly. We now place pie in the freezer for about 40 minutes.

Remove from the freezer and let it rest out the refrigerator for about 15 minutes.

Cut, serve, and enjoy.

Calories | Protein | Fat | Carbs | Fiber | Sodiu...

Calories	Protein	Fat	Carbs	Fiber	Sodiu
430	8.5g	28.2g	13.9g	6g	182mg

Special Hot Chocolate

Cooking Time | Serving

16 min   2

- 2 cups unsweetened almond milk
- 2 teaspoons coconut sugar
- 2 tablespoons of cocoa powder
- 1 teaspoon ground cinnamon
- 1 teaspoon vanilla extract
- Pinch of salt

This is not your ordinary hot chocolate.
In order to enjoy it, place the almond milk in a small saucepan and let it heat for about 7 minutes, stirring occasionally.
Stir in the coconut sugar and cocoa powder until dissolved. Carefully transfer the hot liquid to a blender, along with the cinnamon and vanilla. Blend for 15 seconds until frothy.
Serve immediately and enjoy this hot drink.

Calories	Protein	Fat	Carbs	Fiber	Sodium
280	11.2g	21g	14.8g	6g	222mg

reen Pineapple Smoothie

Cooking Time | Serving

4 min   4

4 cups lightly packed chopped kale leaves stems removed
3/2 cup unsweetened vanilla almond milk or any milk you like
2 frozen medium bananas cut into chunks
1/2 cup plain non-fat Greek yogurt
1/2 cup frozen pineapple pieces
4 tablespoons peanut butter creamy or crunchy (I use natural creamy)
2 to 5 teaspoons honey to taste

Place all ingredients in a blender and blend until smooth. Add more milk to taste if you like a more liquid consistency.

lories	Protein	Fat	Carbs	Fiber	Potassium
223	14g	3g	23g	5g	703mg

Avocado Taste Brownies

Cooking Time | Serving

35 min   15

- 1 cup almond flour
- cocoa powder at the taste
- 1 teaspoon instant coffee
- 1 teaspoon salt
- 4 cups chopped walnuts
- 2 avocados
- 2 apples
- 2 cups sweet potato
- 8 tablespoons ground chia seeds
- 2 teaspoon vanilla
- 1 cup almond butter
- 1 cup coconut butter, softened
- 1/2 cups coconut oil
- 1/2 cups stevia

Heat the oven to 347F, then cover a baking sheet with baking paper.

In a blender, blend the almond flour, cocoa, coffee, cinnamon, salt, and walnuts.

Place the rest of the ingredients in a food processor and blend until the mixture is smooth.

Mix all the ingredients in the same pan and cook for at least 25 minutes

Set aside and let it cool before slicing.

Enjoy.

Calories | Protein | Fat | Carbs |

591.3   11.1g   51g   26.8g

Ginger and Banana Snac

Cooking Time | Serving

50 min   2-4

- 1/2 cup coconut flour
- 3/4 tablespoon grated ginger
- 1 big mature banana
- 1/2 teaspoon baking soda
- melted butter at the taste
- 1 teaspoon cinnamon
- 1 tablespoon apple cider vinegar
- honey at taste
- 1/2 teaspoon ground cardamom
- 3 medium size eggs

Preheat oven to 300F

Prepare a baking plate covered with ba paper

Toss all the ingredients, except for the ba soda and vinegar, in a food processor process until smooth

Now put the baking soda and vinegar in same processor and process again for se seconds

Pour the compote into the baking plate

Bake for 40 minutes in the preheated oven

Enjoy!

Calories | Protein | Car

1407   42g   33

Apricot Almond Cookies

Cooking Time | Serving

50 min   4

- 3/4 cup bran flour (whole wheat)
- 3/4 cup plain flour (white)
- 1/4 cup brown sugar, very firm
- 1 teaspoon baking powder
- 2 eggs, lightly beaten
- 2 tablespoons 1 percent low-fat milk
- 2 tablespoons olive oil
- 2 tablespoons dark honey
- 1/2 teaspoon almond extract
- 3/4 cup chopped dried apricots
- 1/4 cup large chopped almonds

Preheat the oven by starting it at 347F

In a bowl, mix flour, brown sugar, and baking powder.

Mix in the eggs, milk, olive oil, honey, and almond extract until smooth

Stir the mixture with a wooden spoon, adding the chopped almonds and apricots. Knead using floured hands until the ingredients are well integrated into the mixture.

Using your hands, roll out the dough over clingfilm into a rectangular shape, 12 inches long, 3 inches, and about 1 in. high.

Lift the clingfilm and invert the dough onto a nonstick baking sheet.

Bake for 25-30 minutes, until lightly browned.

Transfer to another baking sheet and let cool for 10 minutes. Do not turn off the oven.

Place the cooled dough on a cutting board. With a serrated knife, cut crosswise into 24 portions about 1/2 inch wide.

Place the portions cut side down on the baking sheet and bake again for 15-20 min, until crisp.

Place on a rack and let cool completely.

Store in an airtight container.

Calories	Protein	Fat	Carbs	Fiber	Sodium
75.2	283	2.1g	15.2g	1.1g	17.1mg

uit mix and *Roasted Almonds*

Cooking Time | Serving

60 min   8

1 cup sliced almonds
1 cup unsweetened grated Coconut
2 small pineapples, diced (about 6 cups)
8 oranges, sliced
4 red apples, heartless and cut into dice
2 bananas, peeled, cut in half lengthwise, and sliced crosswise
4 tablespoons of Sherry Cream wine
Fresh mint leaves for decoration

Heat the oven (350F). Once heated, Place the almonds on a baking sheet and bake; stir a few times until they are golden brown and release their aroma, about 10 minutes.

Immediately transfer to a plate to cool. Add the Coconut to the tray and cook, frequently stirring, until lightly browned. Ture, for about 10 minutes.

Immediately transfer to a plate and let cool for at least 10 minutes.

In a bowl, gently mix the pineapple, oranges, apples, banana, and sherry until well blended.

Arrange the fruit mixture evenly in several individual bowls.

Sprinkle evenly with toasted almonds and Coconut, then garnish with mint.

Serve immediately.

lories	Protein	Fat	Carbs	Fiber	Sodium	Cholesterol
172	1.9g	5.3g	31g	6.3g	2.1mg	0.3mg

Fruit Tart

Cooking Time | Serving

40 min   4

- 2 cups fresh raspberries
- 2 cups fresh blueberries
- 4 cups chopped apples
- 2 tablespoons turbinado sugar or brown sugar
- 1 teaspoon ground cinnamon
- 2 teaspoons lemon zest
- 4 teaspoons lemon juice
- 3 tablespoons cornstarch
- For the coating:
- 2 large eggs (egg white only)
- 1/2 cup soy milk
- 1/2 teaspoon salt
- 1 teaspoon vanilla
- 3 tablespoon brown sugar
- whole-wheat pastry flour

Heat oven (350 F).

Sprinkle 1 baking sheet with spray oil.

In a bowl, combine the raspberries, blueberries, apples, sugar, cinnamon, lemon zest, and lemon juice. Stir to mix well.

In the same bowl, add the cornstarch and stir until dissolved.

In a separated bowl, lightly whisk the egg white until foamy. Add the soy milk, salt, vanilla, sugar, and flour, and stir from the bottom up to mix well.

Stir in fruit and starch mixture, combine carefully

Place the mixture in the baking pan prepared earlier.

Bake until tender and topping is golden brown, about 30 minutes. Serve hot.

Enjoy

Calories | Carbs | Fiber | Sodium |

136.2   32g   4.3g   111.2

Sauces, Dips & Dressings

French Vinaigre

Cooking Time | Serving

5 min   2

- 3 and ½ tablespoons apple cider vinegar
- 1 tablespoon finely chopped red onion
- 1 teaspoon balsamic vinegar
- ½ teaspoon dried thyme
- 1 teaspoon mustard
- ¼ cup olive oil
- Salt and black pepper

Mix the apple cider vinegar, onion, and balsa
vinegar in a bowl. Allow standing for 5 minu
Stir in the mustard and thyme. Add the olive
and season with salt and pepper.
Store in an airtight container in the refrigera
for up to 5 days.

Calories | Protein | Fat | Carbs | Fiber | Sodiu

Calories	Protein	Fat	Carbs	Fiber	Sodiu
289	0.5g	31.1g	4.4g	0.6g	210mg

Guacamole

Cooking Time | Serving

11 min   6

- 2 avocados
- ¼ white onion, diced
- 1 cherry tomato, diced
- ¼ cup chopped cilantro
- 2 tablespoons lime juice
- ¼ teaspoon salt
- Ground black pepper

Slice the avocados and tofliere the seed. With
the help of a spoon, separate the pulp from the
skin of the fruit and put everything in a bowl.
Using a fork, mash the fruit pulp until it is an
even consistency. Then add the onion, cilantro,
tomato, lime juice, salt, and pepper.
Mix everything together.
Serve immediately or keep in the refrigerator.

Calories | Protein | Fat | Carbs | Fiber | Sodium |

Calories	Protein	Fat	Carbs	Fiber	Sodium
78	1.3g	6.9g	6.1g	3.2g	79mg

Pineapple Salsa

Cooking Time | Serving

11 min   6-8

460 g fresh diced pineapple
pineapple juice
1 red onion, diced
1 bunch of mint, leaves only,
finely chopped
Salt, to taste

To make great pineapple salsa, mix diced pineapple with its juice, red onion, a bunch of mints, and salt to taste before serving.

You can store the salsa in the refrigerator in an airtight container in order to prevent the proliferation of bacteria for up to 3 days.

Calories | Protein | Fat | Carbs | Fiber | Sodium |

Calories	Protein	Fat	Carbs	Fiber	Sodium
60	1g	0.3g	12g	2g	22mg

Tzatziki

Cooking Time | Serving

14 min   5

- ½ cucumber, cut into julienne strips
- 1 pinch of salt
- 1 cup Greek yogurt
- 8 tablespoons olive oil
- 1 clove of garlic, finely chopped
- 1 tablespoon fresh chopped dill
- 1 teaspoon red wine vinegar
- ½ teaspoon freshly ground black pepper

Inside a blender, chop the cucumber. Place the cucumbers on several layers of paper towels and cover with ½ teaspoon salt. Let dry for about 15 minutes. And with your hands, squeeze out any remaining liquid.

Now take a bowl, and put together cucumber, yogurt, oil, garlic, vinegar, dill, salt, and pepper. Make everything into a smooth mixture.

Before serving, add a couple of tablespoons of olive oil.

Calories | Protein | Fat | Carbs | Fiber | Sodium |

Calories	Protein	Fat	Carbs	Fiber	Sodium
290	4.0g	29.4g	5.4g	0g	650mg

Roman Style Cauliflow

Cooking Time | Serving

12 min   7-8

- 2 thawed or fresh cauliflowers
- ½ cup almond milk (with a pinch of salt)
- 1 and ½ tablespoons apple cider vinegar
- 1 and ½ tablespoons extra virgin olive oil
- ½ clove of garlic
- as much finely chopped fresh parsley as needed
- whole finely chopped shallot
- ½ teaspoon of onion powder
- Anti-inflammatory cookbook for beginners 176
- ½ teaspoon of mustard
- salt to taste
- freshly ground black pepper to taste

To enjoy a great Roman-style cauliflow combine all the ingredients in a blender create a cream.

Serve immediately or transfer to an airti container to store in the refrigerator for up 3 days.

Calories | Protein | Fat | Carbs | Fiber | Sodiu

50   1.2g   4.1g   2.3g   1.5g   162mg

Cucumber and Greek Yogurt Cream

Cooking Time | Serving

8 min   5-6

- 1 cucumber, cut into julienne strips
- a pinch of salt
- 1 cup fat-free Greek yogurt
- 1 1/2 cloves of garlic, finely chopped
- 1 tablespoon extra virgin olive oil
- 1 tablespoon freshly squeezed lemon juice
- ¼ teaspoon freshly ground black pepper

In order to create a sweet cucumber and Greek yogurt cream, start by placing the shredded cucumber in a container and adding salt.

Massage and let it sit for at least 5 minutes. Squeeze the cucumber in order for it to release a liquid. To the liquid, add all the ingredients and mix them until the cream is achieved.

Cover the bowl with plastic wrap and place it in the refrigerator for at least 2 hours for the flavors to blend. Then serve as you like!

Calories | Protein | Fat | Carbs | Sodium |

50   5g   2.1g   2.9g   112mg

pple Sauce

Cooking Time | Serving

10 min   2

1/2 cup low-fat cottage cheese
1/2 cup unsweetened apple juice
1 teaspoon cinnamon
3 tablespoons roasted almonds

Combine the cottage cheese and apple juice in a bowl, and mix well.
Sprinkle with cinnamon and keep mixing well
Top with almonds
Take the spoon and enjoy.

lories | Protein | Fat | Carbs |

233   16.22g   14.13g   8.51g

Avocado Cream

Cooking Time | Serving

5 min   1

- 1 avocado, cut in half and pitted
- ¼ cup whole coconut milk
- Juice of 1 lime
- ¼ teaspoon salt
- ¼ cup fresh coriander leaves

Process the avocado pulp with a food processor. Add the coconut milk, lime juice, salt, and coriander and blend until smooth and creamy.

Calories | Protein | Fat | Carbs | Fiber | Sugar | Cholesterol |

Calories	Protein	Fat	Carbs	Fiber	Sugar	Cholesterol
122	2g	11g	7g	4g	2g	0

Vegan Caesar Dressing Zes

Cooking Time | Serving

10 min   1

- ¼ cup tahini
- 1 teaspoon mustard
- Juice of 1 lemon
- 2 teaspoons capers, chopped
- 3 cloves garlic, chopped
- 1 teaspoon maple syrup
- ½ teaspoon salt
- ½ teaspoon freshly ground black pepper
- 1 or 2 tablespoons cold water

Mix tahini, mustard, lemon juice, capers, ga maple syrup, salt, and pepper in a medi bowl.
Add water 1 tablespoon at a time if necessar dilute the dressing to a pourable consistenc

Calories	Protein	Fat	Carbs	Fiber	Sugar	Cholester
82	2g	7g	5g	1g	1g	0

Simple Citrus Fruit Vinaigrette Dressing

Cooking Time | Serving

10 min   1

- Juice of 1 lemon
- 2 tablespoons apple cider vinegar
- 2 tablespoons olive oil
- ½ teaspoon mustard
- 1 clove of minced garlic
- ¾ teaspoon salt
- 1 teaspoon freshly ground black pepper
- ½ teaspoon dried oregano
- ½ teaspoon dried thyme

Mix the lemon juice, vinegar, oil, mustard, garlic, salt, pepper, oregano, and thyme in a medium bowl.
Serve.

Calories	Protein	Fat	Carbs	Fiber	Sugar	Cholesterol
54	0g	5g	1g	0	283	0

Dijon Lemon Dressing

Cooking Time | Serving

10 min   13

¼ cup olive oil
1 teaspoon mustard
½ teaspoon honey, raw
¼ teaspoon basil
1 clove of garlic, minced
¼ teaspoon sea salt, fine
2 tablespoons lemon juice, fresh

Mix all ingredients and shake vigorously. Store in the refrigerator for up to one week.

Calories | Protein | Fat | Carbs |

128   0.1g   1.8g   1.8g

Pistachio Pesto

Cooking Time | Serving

5 min   4

- 2 cups basil leaves, fresh and well-packed
- 1 cup pistachios, raw
- ½ cup olive oil, divided
- ½ cup Parmesan cheese, shredded
- 2 teaspoons lemon juice, fresh
- ½ teaspoon garlic powder
- Sea salt and black pepper to taste

Take out the food processor, and blend together the basil, pistachios, and a quarter cup of olive oil for fifteen seconds. Add the cheese, lemon juice, and garlic powder, and season with salt and pepper. Pour in the rest of the olive oil and make sure it is well blended.

Serve immediately and keep in the fridge for four days.

Calories | Protein | Fat | Carbs |

229   5.5g   3.6g   3.8g

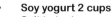

Soy Tender D

Cooking Time | Serving

24 hours　　　　　2

- Soy yogurt 2 cups
- Salt to taste
- Chives (or other herbs and/or spices to taste)

Nutritionist's advice

In a healthy diet, this tasty spread helps
health and well-being of our intestines as v
as being suitable for a balanced vegan diet.
The presence of soy, contrary to what '
previously thought, is very indicated in th
women suffering from breast cancer,
also from other estrogen-related disea
(endometriosis, fibrocystic mastopathy,
fibroids of the uterus).

Procedure:

Take a funnel and place it over a tall cup, lir
with a cloth of linen or cheese gauze and p
in the yogurt.
Let it sit in the refrigerator for 24 hours, du
which time the yogurt will lose some of its lic
(empty the collection container if necessary
When finished, pour the yogurt into a b
and add salt and flavor with fresh herbs a
or spices (chives, pepper, curry, paprika, ga
etc., to taste).

5-Weeks
Meal Plan

Week

	Breakfast	Lunch	Dinner	Dessert
Monday	Salty muffin	Indian spinach soup with crunchy bread	Salmon in green	Blueberry and oat crisp bars
Tuesday	Matcha Tea Latte	Lemon poultry grill	Broccoli and cauliflower salad	Apricot Almond Cookies
Wednesday	Turkish Milk	Salmon cooked icon rosemary and walnuts	Vegan Burritos	Maple syrup and cranberry protein bars.
Thursday	Banana, quinoa and clove mix	Italian Grilled Shrimps	Tasty Coconut Chicken	purple fruit mix
Friday	Coconut and green apple porridge	Bronte's baked fish	Swordfish carpaccio	Green Pineapple smoothie
Saturday	Apple Jam	Carrots with orange and honey glaze	Chicken Pita	Lemony & Blackberry Granita
Sunday	Eggs with Zucchini Noodles	Carrots with orange and honey glazeSmoked salmon on cucumber rounds	Light chicken with vegetables	Carrot energy bars

Week 2

	Breakfast	Lunch	Dinner	Dessert
Monday	Carrot cake	Lentil soup	Scallops	Special hot chocolate
Tuesday	Omelette	Vegan Bowls	Grilled Salmon	Tasty berry tarts
Wednesday	Turkish Milk	Salmon cooked icon rosemary and walnuts		Fantastic chia seed and cocoa pudding
Thursday	Vegan bowl with hummus and avocado	Zucchini noodles with king prawns.	Orzo shrimp salad	Fruit smoothie and matcha
Friday	Blueberry breakfast bowl	Seafood Stuffed Pasta shells	Pork fillet with garlic and lemon	Avocado ,cherry and spinach smoothie
Saturday	Oats with banana and dates	Cauliflower pizzas	Reinterpreted Israeli Couscous	Avocado taste brownies
Sunday	Breakfast with quinoa and raisins	Tuna and Olive Salad Sandwiches	Crab soup	Ginger and banana snacks

Week 3

	Breakfast	Lunch	Dinner	Dessert
Monday	Fruit and vegetable smoothie	Tuna and Olive Salad Sandwiches	Tuna salad	cranberry and quinoa energy bars
Tuesday	Matcha Tea Latte	Lemon poultry grill	Marinated Shrimp Salad with avocado	Spiced Pecans nuts
Wednesday	Banana, quinoa and clove mix	Salmon cooked icon rosemary and walnuts	Saltimbocca of chicken and sage	Cold mango and coconut cake
Thursday	Oats with banana and dates	Vegan Chickpea Wraps	Gourmet Tuna Patties	Carrot energy bars
Friday	Apple Jam	Cabbage, quinoa and avocado salad	Vegetarian Burgers	Camomile-based regenerate
Saturday	Omelette	Sunrise Salmon	Avocado gremolata Salmon	Maple syrup and cranberry protein bars.
Sunday	Salty muffin	Vegetarian carbonara	Tasty Coconut Chicken	Special scrumbled eggs

Week 4

	Breakfast	Lunch	Dinner	Dessert
Monday	Coconut and green apple porridge	Bronte's baked fish	Honey chicken steak	Blueberry and oat crisp bars
Tuesday	Turkish Milk	Vegetables Piadina	Scallops	Spiced Pecans nuts
Wednesday	Carrot cake	Herbed Chicken Pasta	Swordfish carpaccio	Avocado ,cherry and spinach smoothie
Thursday	Blueberry breakfast bowl	Bagna Cauda green Salmon	Grilled Salmon	purple fruit mix
Friday	Salty muffin	Indian spinach soup with crunchy bread	bowl of corn, shrimp and cherry tomatoes	Avocado taste brownies
Saturday	Banana, quinoa and clove mix	Avocado chicken salad	Salmon in green	Green Pineapple smoothie
Sunday	Eggs with Zucchini Noodles	Lemon poultry grill	Rivisited Israeli Couscous	Special scrumbled eggs

Week

	Breakfast	Lunch	Dinner	Dessert
Monday	Salty muffin	Tuna and Olive Salad Sandwiches	Vegan Burritos	cranberry and quinoa energy bars
Tuesday	Vegan bowl with hummus and avocado	Smoked salmon on cucumber rounds	Spicy Chicken legs	Camomile-based regenerate
Wednesday	Matcha Tea Latte	Lentil soup	Broccoli and cauliflower salad	Blueberry and oat crisp bars
Thursday	Apple Jam	Carrots with orange and honey glaze	Chicken Pita	Cold mango and coconut cake
Friday	Carrot cake	Alfredo chicken burgers	Light chicken with vegetables	Ginger and banana snacks
Saturday	Turkish Milk	Vegan Bowls	Tuna salad	Avocado taste brownies
Sunday	Coconut and green apple porridge	Salmon cooked icon rosemary and walnuts	Orzo shrimp salad	Carrot energy bars

Alphabetic Index

A

Amazing Berry-Almond Smoothie — 97
Amazing Cauliflower & Potato Curry Soup — 64
Apple Jam — 95
Apple Omelet — 77
Apricot Almond Cookies — 107
Avocado, Cherry, and Spinach Smoothie — 100
Avocado Chicken Salad — 47
Avocado Cream — 113
Avocado Gremolata Salmon — 31

B

Baked Chicken with Zucchini — 52
Breakfast with Mashed Cauliflower — 80
Bronte's Baked Fish — 38
Brown Rice Salad — 89
Brown Rice with Blueberries and Coconut — 103
Bruxelles Roasted Salmon — 29

C

Cabbage and Olives Sautéed Salad — 24
Calories I Protein I Fat I Carbs I Fiber I Sodium I — 23
Carrot Energy Bars — 98
Carrots with Orange and Honey Glaze — 25
Casserole with Green Beans — 12
Celery, Turnip, and Artichoke Soup Creme — 9
Chia Seeds Porridge — 91
Chicken Breast Soup — 68
Chicken Pita — 57
Chickpeas and Cauliflower Casserole — 11
Chickpeas Couscous — 48
Coconut and Green Apple Porridge — 81
Coconut Rice with Berries — 94
Cold Mango and Coconut Cake — 104
Crab Soup — 36

F

Fantastic Chia Seed and Cocoa Pudding — 101
Fennel and Pumpkin Risotto — 8
French Vinaigrette — 110
Fresh Cucumber Soup — 73
Fresh Salmon wraps — 39
Fruit Smoothie and Matcha — 99

G

Garlic Scented Shrimps with Creamy Mushrooms Side — 34
Ginger and Banana Snacks — 106
Glazed Chicken with Date Chutney — 54
Gourmet Salad — 60
Greek Special Roasted Chicken — 44
Grilled Catfish Sandwich — 37
Grilled Chicken with Orange and Avocado — 50
Grilled Vegetable Chicken Kebab — 56
Ham Muffins — 85
Herbed Chicken Pasta — 20
Herbed-Mustard-Coated Pork Tenderloin — 55

I

Italian Grilled Shrimps — 40

K

Kefir and Berries Oats — 90

L

Lean Green Broccoli Tacos — 13
Lentil Flour and Zucchini Crepes — 22
Lentils and Rice Mediterranean Soup — 61
Lettuce and Chicken Strips Salad — 46

M

Marsala Chicken — 51
Mediterranean Bowl — 69
Mediterranean Green Beans — 70

Mustard Lentil Pate — 21

O

Oats with Banana and Dates — 82
Omelet — 84
Onion and Orange Salad — 71
Orzo Shrimp Salad — 41

P

Pan-Fried Zucchini and Quinoa — 88
Pasta al Pesto with Light Chicken and Vegetables — 45
Pistachio Pesto — 115
Poached egg - Avocado - Salmon Toast — 92

R

Roasted Beetroot Hummus — 66
Roman-Style Cauliflower — 112

S

Salmon Balls — 33
Salmon Cooked Icon Rosemary and Walnuts — 27
Salmon in Green — 28
Saltimbocca of Chicken and Sage — 53
Savoy Cabbage Lasagna with Porcini Mushrooms — 10
Scrambled Eggs with Cabbage — 79
Seafood Stuffed Pasta Shells — 32
Soy Tender Dip — 116
Special Hot Chocolate — 105
Spicy Chicken Legs — 58
Spicy Chicken with Carrots — 49
Spicy Turmeric Flakes — 72
Spinach Salad with Roasted Sweet Potatoes, White Beans, and Basil — 65
Spinach Salad with Soy and Ginger Dressing — 67
Stuffed potatoes — 16
Sweet-Sour Salmon — 35

T

Tasty Berry Tarts — 102
Tuna and Spinach Salad — 63
Tuna Salad — 86
Turkish Milk — 78
Tzatziki — 111

V

Vegan Bowls — 19
Vegan Bowl with Hummus and Avocado — 83
Vegan Caesar Dressing Zesty — 114
Vegan Chickpea Wraps — 18
Vegan Coleslaw — 74
Vegan Sandwiches — 17
Vegetables and Mushrooms Wrap — 14
Vegetarian Pita — 15
Vegetarian Roast — 23
Vegetarian Savory Pie — 87

W

Watermelon Fresh Salad — 62

Y

Yogurt, Berries, and Nuts Parfait — 93

Z

Zucchini Noodles with King Prawns — 30

Printed in Great Britain
by Amazon

87064085R20071